UNIVERSITY OF NORTH CAROLINA AT CHAPEL HILL
DEPARTMENT OF ROMANCE LANGUAGES

NORTH CAROLINA STUDIES
IN THE ROMANCE LANGUAGES AND LITERATURES

ESSAYS; TEXTS, TEXTUAL STUDIES AND TRANSLATIONS; SYMPOSIA

Founder: URBAN TIGNER HOLMES

Distributed by:

UNIVERSITY OF NORTH CAROLINA PRESS
CHAPEL HILL
North Carolina 27514
U.S.A.

NORTH CAROLINA STUDIES IN THE
ROMANCE LANGUAGES AND LITERATURES

Essays

Number 5

POETRY AND ANTIPOETRY:
A STUDY OF SELECTED ASPECTS OF MAX JACOB'S POETIC STYLE

POETRY AND ANTIPOETRY:
A STUDY OF SELECTED ASPECTS OF MAX JACOB'S POETIC STYLE

BY

ANNETTE THAU

CHAPEL HILL

NORTH CAROLINA STUDIES IN THE ROMANCE
LANGUAGES AND LITERATURES
U.N.C. DEPARTMENT OF ROMANCE LANGUAGES
1976

Library of Congress Cataloging in Publication Data

Thau, Annette.
 Poetry and antipoetry.

 (North Carolina studies in the Romance languages and literatures)
 Bibliography: p. 114.
 Includes index.
 1. Jacob, Max, 1876-1944—Style. I. Title. II. Series.

PQ2619.A17Z87 841'.9'12 74-32437

ISBN: 9780807891704

depósito legal: v. 4.197 - 1975

artes gráficas soler, s. a. - jávea, 28 - valencia (8) - 1976

I would like to dedicate this book to my husband, Fred, and to my two sons, Robert and Stephen.

Tout est dit, et tout est poétique
(MAX JACOB about VILLON)

CONTENTS

	Pages
INTRODUCTION	15
CHAPTER	
I. PLAY WITH WORDS AND SOUNDS	21
Puns	22
Puns with a single reference	23
Paronomasia	30
Based on the repetition of the same word	31
Based on the repetition of homonyms and homophones	33
Sound links	38
II. THE CLICHE IN PARODY	50
Satirical parody	52
Creative parodies	60
III. IMAGERY	70
Literal Imagery	70
Substantives effective in a number of ways at once.	70
Oneiric imagery	82
Figurative imagery	91
Simile	91
Metaphor	99
CONCLUSION	110
BIBLIOGRAPHY	114
LIST OF POEMS ANALYSED	126

NOTE: I have used the following abbreviations throughout the book. References are to the editions indicated.

CD.   *Le Cornet à dés* (Paris, 1945).
CD, II. *Le Cornet à dés, II* (Paris, 1955).
DP.   *Derniers poèmes en vers et en prose* (Paris, 1961)
DT.   *La Défense de Tartufe* (Paris, 1964).
FddL.   *Fond de l'eau* (Paris, 1927).
HdC.   *L'Homme de cristal* (Paris, 1946).
LC.   *Le Laboratoire central* (Paris, 1960).
PMR.   *Les Pénitents en maillots roses* (Paris, 1925).
MC.   *Morceaux choisis* (Paris, 1936).
SI.   *Sacrifice Impérial* (in MC).
SM.   *Saint Matorel*, roman, suivi des *Œuvres burlesques et mystiques de Frère Matorel* et du *Siège de Jérusalem* (Paris, 1936).
VI.   *Visions infernales* (Paris, 1924).

ACKNOWLEDGMENT

I would like to thank the individuals who helped to make this study possible. I would particularly like to acknowledge my debt to Michael Riffaterre who read early versions of this manuscript and made many helpful suggestions; and to Leroy C. Breunig and Leon Roudiez whose comments of an early draft were also most helpful.

I would also like to thank the French department of Barnard College for allowing me to consult the unpublished Mespoulet file.

INTRODUCTION

Although Max Jacob is now regarded as one of the major French poets of the twentieth century, only limited aspects of his poetry have received critical attention. Much of the considerable critical literature concerning Jacob dwells on his extraordinary personality. Published studies of his poetry are fragmentary or concentrate on aspects of his early volumes characterized variously as cubist or hermetic or the like. These studies fail to convey the complexity and variety of Jacob's poetry, or its range. In an unpublished letter to Mlle. Marguerite Mespoulet, Jacob identified three tendencies in his work: *"humour"* (wit), *"amour"* (love, lyrical elements), and *"inconscience"* (chance, the subconscious). He added that these three had always coexisted, but that, early in his career, in the *rue Ravignan* days (when Jacob's painter friends and close associates were creating cubism), he had been drawn by his entourage in the direction of *"inconscience"* whereas later *"humour amour"* dominated. This statement accurately describes Jacob's evolution as a poet. More importantly it identifies tendencies which were present at every stage of his long and prolific poetic career. In most volumes of his poetry, and indeed in many poems, these three tendencies coexist. To explore Jacob's art as a poet fully, one must study the stylistic features of his poetry — not merely those used in the early works that made his reputation but those that characterize his entire poetic output.

The methods and aims of this book are to identify the principal structures (that is, the principal stylistic devices) employed by Jacob in his poetry; and to study these in themselves and their effects in larger poetic sequences. I have analysed each structure in two contexts: as a fragment of a poem (in the title, for example, or in one line or phrase); and as the main element of a long poetic passage or of an entire poem, where the structure under consideration determines the total effect of the passage or poem. I have been concerned with how the texts "work," rather than with their interpretation or evaluation, and I have sought to remain as objective as possible by restricting discussion to what Wimsatt and Beardsley have called "internal" or "public" evidence,[1] that is, the meaning of words, the syntax of a poem, or the meaning of the poems or images so far as it can be inferred directly from the texts themselves.

Structures were selected on the principles enunciated by Leo Spitzer[2] and Michael Riffaterre.[3] After careful readings of the texts to determine what structures appeared most expressive, I sought to confirm my intuition of the importance of these structures through rereadings, using additional criteria. The recurrence of a given structure in different contexts identified it as a constant in the author's style. Frequent critical commentary on a particular feature of a writer's style, regardless of the nature of the commentary, was taken to reflect the stylistic importance of that aspect of the text receiving commentary.[4] The convergence of a number of stylistic features in a segment of a text was taken as an indication that the author was directing the reader's attention to that segment of the text.[5] I therefore selected for analysis two structures which have elicited frequent discussion — play with words or sounds and parodies — and a third one that critics have usually overlooked — Jacob's imagery.

Analysis revealed one problem to be central. The critical literature on Jacob condemns a number of aspects of his poetry, chiefly those associated with elements of play and humor. Those

---

[1] W. K. Wimsatt, Jr. and Monroe C. Beardsley, "The Intentional Fallacy," *The Verbal Icon* (The University of Kentucky Press, 1954), p. 11.
[2] See *Linguistics and Literary History* (New York, 1962), pp. 1-27.
[3] See *Le Style des Pléiades de Gobineau* (New York, 1957), as well as other articles listed in the bibliography.
[4] This principle was formulated by Riffaterre. See in particular "Criteria for Style Analysis," *Word*, XV (1959), pp. 154-174; and "L'Etude stylistique des formes conventionnelles," *The French Review*, XXXVIII, No. 1 (Oct. 1964), pp. 3-14.
[5] See *Le Style des Pléiades de Gobineau*, p. 20.

elements analysed in my first chapter as "association of words on the basis of "sounds" have particularly aroused the ire of critics. Yet, a number of them have been so struck by Jacob's verbal play that they have ignored almost everything else in his poetry and remember him only as the poet who wrote poems based on association of sounds, characterized variously as "outrageous verbal acrobatics," [6] "avowedly destructive," [7] "plutôt laborieux," [8] "de la jonglerie verbale," [9] "[de la] nigauderie pour rire." [10] These critics have not articulated the reasons for their objection to this type of verbal play in poetry. But it is clear that Jacob's poems violate their expectations of what a poem is or should be. The concept underlying this attitude is a variation of the classic injunction against mixtures of style, based on the assumption that there are, or ought to be, distinctions between the noble or elevated style of poetry or tragedy and a low style in which humor may be used. [11] Jacob's use of playful structures as elements of his poetic style is thus considered by critics as too vulgar, or too frivolous, and hence destructive: in a word, "anti-poetic."

These objections are related to another aspect of Jacob's style, identified by Gabriel Bounoure: namely, the dissociation between poetry and beauty, and the fact that Jacob's poetic language or level of style is devoid of poetic diction — indeed, at times, close to the vernacular. [12] Clichés, snatches of conversation, ordinary, even pedestrian objects, and the like dominate many poems. This gives his poetry a surface appearance of banality, possibly of triviality. Again, this may appear "anti-poetic."

Yet it ought to be evident that one cannot isolate those aspects considered "anti-poetic" from the rest of Jacob's work, or from the rest of a poem. The very fact that these aspects have been singled out for criticism or are considered by some as the central element of Jacob's poetry underlines their importance.

---

[6] S. J. Collier, "Max Jacob and the poème en prose," *MLR*, LI (oct. 1956), 522.
[7] Georges Lemaître, quoted by Collier, *ibid.*
[8] Hubert Fabureau, *Max Jacob* (Paris, 1935), p. 65.
[9] Suzanne Bernard, *Le Boème en prose de Baudelaire jusqu'à nos jours* (Paris, 1935), p. 65.
[10] Yvon Belaval, *La Rencontre avec Max Jacob* (Paris, 1946), p. 91.
[11] See Erich Auerbach, *Mimesis* (New York, 1953).
[12] Untitled review, *NRF*, XXXXIII (July 1, 1934), p. 109.

One can meet these critical objections only by analysing impartially and objectively the function of Jacob's structures, and by regarding poetry as, among other things, a special use of words that seeks to extend them beyond their ordinary dimensions, so as to reveal unsuspected meaning. The element of obscurity, or mystery, which is an integral aspect of Jacob's poetry, is hence viewed as a necessary concomitant to the particular use of language in a given text. From this view, any structure that renews the reader's perception of language and reality, whether it involves the use of nonsense, fantasy, anti-rational and prosaic elements, chance, etc, or the use of more traditional figures such as imagery, is intrinsically poetic, and therefore, legitimate. The poetic value of a structure is judged by criteria related to such questions as: How is this structure used in this text? In what way is the meaning of a word enriched or a new meaning created? What precisely adds the element of surprise or mystery? What gives new or unexpected dimension to a text? Can it be read on a number of levels? and the like.

It has been said that Jacob deliberately mystified his readers, that nothing in the poems is what it seems to be. This is not always a pejorative judgment, but rather, as the two citations below make clear, a characterization of Jacob's poetic universe, a recognition of the importance of the element of ambiguity in his poetry: "Nevertheless, you think that you know where you are, that you can orient yourself. You recognize words or fragments of sentences. They are not strangers to you. You have seen them, or phrases similar to them, in the newspaper. They look familiar. You wade in, recklessly and suddenly lose your footing. At the very instant when you seem to grasp the meaning, to seize through his language the very essence of the poet, his personality, his path, something strange explodes, like a rocket or an infernal machine."[13] "There is almost always, in Jacob's work, the intention to mystify, that is, a need for gratuitous invention, without reference to reality, or (more often) with an apparent realism which is only a trap, and the finished poem *must* deceive because

---

[13] Pierre Lagarde, *Max Jacob, mystique et martyr*, Paris, 1944, p. 14. (My translation).

it is never, either literarily or morally, what it seems to be." [14] Ordinary objects or scenes — such as a wheelbarrow, a hole in the wall, a corn on one's foot — appear in the poems only to mislead the reader into thinking he is reading about a familiar, mundane world. Invariably, however, another dimension intrudes, or is revealed. The structures which contribute the most to this effect of ambiguity or mystification are a function of Jacob's use of imagery. They are also intimately linked to his "anti-poetic" structures, especially play with words or sounds, and parodies. These do not, however, result uniquely in effects of humor or ambiguity, as has been assumed implicitly or explicitly by Jacob's critics. All structures may have a variety of effects, depending on their contexts, a characteristic which has been called by Riffaterre "le caractère polyvalent du procédé de style." [15]

One final note. Jacob's poetic output is divided into prose and verse. This raises some delicate questions, mainly because a precise definition of the prose poem has yet to be established. A number of general tendencies are more readily identified with Jacob's prose poetry than with his verse poetry: in prose poems, the "I" tends to be absent from lyrical contexts, resulting in more "objective" poems; humorous contexts are frequently associated with effects of nonsense, fantasy, or ambiguity in that the reader often has to invent varying interpretations. These distinctions are far from absolute, however. Nor do they necessarily hold for anyone other than Jacob. As used herein, prose poetry and verse poetry indicate only typographical disposition, "verse poetry" designating poetry presenting itself in separate lines *(vers)*, whether free or based on conventional syllable counts; and "prose poetry" designating poetry presenting itself in paragraphs, or in the case of very brief poems, in run-on phrases or sentences. [16]

---

[14] Marcel Raymond, *De Baudelaire au surréalisme* (Paris, 1952), p. 255. (My translation).

[15] *Le Style des Pléiades de Gobineau*, p. 211.

[16] Since this study was completed, the publication of a comprehensive series of *Cahiers* dealing with Max Jacob has been undertaken, under the auspices of *La Revue des Lettres Modernes*. So far, one *Cahier*, entitled "autour du poème en prose," has been published (August, 1973). René Plantier has also published a study entitled *Max Jacob* (Desclée de Brouwer, 1972), defining Jacob's religious beliefs. These studies were published too late for me to use them in the preparation of this manuscript, but the

interested reader will find that they amplify a number of aspects of Max Jacob's poetic style ("L'écriture du rêve dans le *Cornet à dés*," "La mythologie dans l'œuvre poétique de Max Jacob," the presence of the devil in his universe) studied in the third chapter of this book, imagery.

CHAPTER I *

PLAY WITH WORDS AND SOUNDS

Word and sound play have been prominent in a number of literatures: the classical Hindu, the Elizabethan, and the medieval. In an effort to endow language with new possibilities, twentieth century French poets as diverse as Cocteau, the surrealists, and Claudel, have introduced sound and word play into their poetry in ways that recall earlier traditions. Occult tradition holds that there is a fundamental analogy between the structure of the universe and the structure of language and that, therefore a necessary affinity exists between the sound of a word and its meaning. Cocteau analysed the significance of puns in Jacob's work in terms which recall this tradition, stating: "Often, mysteriously moved by a random association of words *("coq à l'âne")* by Max Jacob, I am reminded of the tradition of puns of the oracles of Delphi, of Delos, of Dodona..." [1] Breton, in more literary terms, has pointed out that verbal play allows chance to erupt in the poem. He also saw in verbal play a manifestation of the *"automatisme"* he favored which permits the poet to abdicate rational control, to come into contact with the irrational (as in "automatic writing" and the puns of Desnos). This interpretation of puns reflects the preoccupations of the surrealists. Claudel saw in language itself a hidden kind of knowledge reminiscent of Philippe de Thaon and the medieval view of

---

* Substantial portions of this chapter first appeared in *La Revue des Lettres Modernes*, Nos. 336-339 (Paris, 1973), *Max Jacob I*, pp. 125-156.

[1] Jean Cocteau, "Max Jacob," *Le Disque Vert*, 2ème année, No. 2 (Nov. (1923), 30. (my translation).

etymologies which accorded scientific validity to popular etymologies. Finally, in a more diffuse way, verbal play in poetry supports the definition of poetry as an exploration of all the possibilities inherent in words. Such play both conceals and reveals unsuspected mystery and, through exploration in depth, forces reconsideration of both the words used, and the objects represented.

These various orientations are all found in Jacob's poetry, where they manifest themselves in structures exhibiting a bewildering variety of patterns of organization, both syntactical and semantic. I have divided this chapter into two sections which correspond to a general distinction between puns (word play based on distinctions of meaning) and sound links (word play based on patterns of sounds).

Puns

There are two essential conditions which define the pun. One is the existence of multiple and disparate meanings for a word. The other is a context that permits the application of two or more of these meanings. The source of the pun's potential, the contrast afforded by multiple meanings of a single word, defines its limitations as well. The pun exploits existing meanings. Semantic usage which results in distinctions between nuances of words or the creation of new meanings cannot be said to result in puns — although in contexts where a figurative meaning is superimposed (either because the context of the pun is an image, or because one of the appropriate pun meanings is figurative), the potentialities of the pun word are greatly multiplied. The pun's potential effects are thus as varied as the contexts in which it appears — from the broadly farcical to the subtly witty, from the comic to the lyric. Theoreticians of the pun have long considered it semi-metaphorical. Unlike metaphor, however, the pun cannot be said to be ambiguous; it cannot be said to be obscure. The only possible ambiguity is the momentary balancing of possible meanings as one becomes aware of the pun. Once it is recognized that more than one meaning fits, however, this ambiguity is dissolved (unless the context itself is ambiguous). The pun's effect is derived from the recognition of its multiple meanings as equally applicable to a particular context. The text's control of interpretation is complete.

The pun occurs in two syntactical patterns. The pun word can be stated once (puns with a single reference), or it can be repeated (paronomasia). A pun with a single reference is a means of making two statements, often totally unrelated, with one word or phrase, whereas paronomasia results in a shift or contrast in meaning. This results in differences in the function of the pun within the poem. Each is therefore considered separately.

Puns with a single reference.

The context of a pun, its location in the poem (in the title, the body of the poem, or the conclusion), affects both its structural function in the poem and its meaning.

The multiple meanings of the pun word in a title suggest the theme or imagery of the poem, or both, as in the poem entitled "Terre arrosée" (LC, p. 88). The title means literally, "earth which has been watered." *Arrosée* also suggests its homophone, *à rosée*, meaning "at the time of dew, at dawn." The perception of this homophone may occur retroactively, after reading the first line of the poem:

> Dans les verts brouillards de l'Aurore

The dual theme of the dawn and of the dew is carried through in the imagery of the poem, especially the second stanza:

> La nuit quand je pense à la poésie
> Je ne peux pas, je ne peux pas dormir
> Eau d'aurore
> Les mots, ne les dissipez pas encore
> —Tu les trouveras dans la rue
> En allant revoir tes amis:
> Entre le grand ciel triste et tout ce qui, gonflé,
> Soupire, le miracle naîtra de la terre arrosée.

The juxtaposition of "tu les trouveras dans la rue" ("the words which become a poem") and the lines which follow suggests an analogy between the genesis of a poem in the mind of the poet and the genesis of any living thing, both equally mysterious forms of creation subject to the same fundamental laws. The word "miracle" in the last line makes this theme explicit. This analogy further suggests a symbolic meaning for the title, since the final line unites two traditional poetic themes: that of water as a fecundating principle, and of the dawn as a time for rebirth, both united in the image of "Terre arrosée". The implication is that the poet, like the earth, is renewed by the dew and the dawn.

Occasionally, the pun in a title is based on an unusual meaning of a word, with the result that the poem functions as a metalinguistic commentary. This is true, for example, of "Petit essai sur le diable," in CD, II, p. 52:

> On appelle diable une sorte de brouette en fer dont on se sert dans les gares. On ne la nomme pas ainsi parcequ'elle fait, comme on dit un bruit de tous les diables; en effet, le diable est silencieux mais parce que son extrémité est amincie comme une pelle afin de happer les marchandises comme le diable nous happe.

Diable as Jacob explains in the first sentence, can designate, not only the devil, but also a two wheeled trolley that is used by railway porters as a luggage truck. In this poem, Jacob links this unusual meaning of *diable* to its more ordinary meaning through a whimsical etymology, motivated by an equally whimsical analogy between the characteristics of the trolley and those of the devil. The humorous use of the expression "un bruit de tous les diables" provides Jacob with an additional pun since the figurative *diable* is given a literal interpretation, which further reinforces the etymology. Modern semantics and semiotics stress that the meaning of a word is "arbitrary," that it is the result of accidental phonological development, and independent of it. This poem on the other hand suggests, through the use of fantasy, that the evolution of meaning is logical since the different meanings of a single word, *diable*, result, not from accident, but from the fact that the word reveals the true nature of both objects. Two meanings are enshrined in one word because, at a deeper level of reality, there is a fundamental analogy between them. This leaves the impression that probing language will reveal non-linguistic realities.

Jacob's etymological puns are generally fanciful, as in the above example. In one instance, however, the etymological meaning of a word is restored to it through the structure of the poem, entitled "Poème." (CD, p. 38):

> "Que veux-tu de moi, dit Mercure. —Ton sourire et tes dents, dit Vénus. —Elles sont fausses. Que veux-tu de moi? —Ton caducée. —Je ne m'en sépare point. —Viens l'apporter ici, divin facteur." / Il faut lire cela dans le texte grec: cela s'appelle Idylle. Au collège, un ami, souvent refusé aux examens, me dit: "Si on traduisait en grec un roman de Daudet, on serait assez fort après pour l'examen! mais je ne peux pas travailler la nuit. Ca fait pleurer ma mère." Il faut lire aussi cela dans le texte grec, messieurs; c'est une idylle, ειδυλλος, petit tableau.

The etymology of the word *idylle* quoted in the final line of text is exact. It provides a link between the two sections of the poem, as a kind of metalinguistic commentary. The first section of the poem, through "divin facteur," has some of the conventional elements of an idyll in the general sense the word has acquired: a poem dealing with a love story. The second section of the poem is an idyll in the etymological sense of the word: a little tableau. The implication is that either section of the poem consitutes an idyll in the primitive sense of the word.

Instead of starting out with a pun, the poem can lead up to one. Those poems are generally witty or comic. The conclusion of one very brief piece in CD, II, p. 52, also entitled "Petit essai sur le diable," states that at a performance of the *Opéra*, "...l'orchestre réclama des diables sur des plaques de fer. Il paraît que les diables vinrent en personnes." "En personnes" can mean either: "it seems that the devils came personally" or "it seems that the devils came costumed (disguised) as people." In this instance, the pun effect is due to a change in number of the word *personne*, singular in the expression *en personne* and plural in Jacob's coined phrase.

Within the body of the poem, the pun plays various roles. It suggests a number of different readings of a line, as in the following two lines, from "De Terre en ciel," in HdC, p. 20:

> Il nous invita sur ses Terres
> hoirs...

The antecedent of "Il" is the Deity. This is unusual in that two separate words, *terres* and *hoirs,* are yoked together to suggest a homophone: *terroirs*. *Terroirs* is not exactly synonymous with *terres*. It means "land," but is an affective term, generally singular, which affectionately designates the region of one's birth. It is also an agricultural term, meaning "fertile land." The separation between *terres* and *hoirs,* emphasized further by the *enjambement* and the archaic meanings of *hoirs* ("heirs") emphasizes the separate meanings of each possible reading: "He left us on these lands" or "He left us on these lands, heirs." Moreover, the distinctions between these readings stress the varying affective connotations of "terres," "terroir," and "hoirs."

"Le Dernier Calembour," in HdC (pp. 97-98), contains a more complex example. Two possible meanings of *aimant*, "loving" or "magnet," are the focal point of the poem.

"J'irai vers le rocher dont parlent les poètes
"Avec l'arbre d'oubli sur mes barques de fête
"Aimant l'aimant d'amour Dieu saura si je l'aime!"
Volant par les cheveux tout ce qui fut de fer:
armures des soldats, lances, ferrures, emblèmes
et l'ancre qu'on jetait sur le fond du problème
l'Aimant Dieu, l'aimant videra les cimetières. [2]

Each homonym designates various qualities that Jacob attributes to the Deity: he is loving; he acts as a magnet, both literally, drawing all iron to him, and figuratively, giving love, attracting love. The various objects of iron named — *armures de soldats, lances* — express the final reconciliation on the day of judgment when "swords shall be beaten into plowshares." Each time the word *aimant* is used, either or both meanings fit, so that the repetition of the term multiplies the possible combinations of meanings. Therefore, the first line containing the pun can be read in the following ways: "The loving, the magnet of Love, God will know if I love him"; "I, loving the magnet of love, God will know if I

---

[2] Note the additional pun on *encre* (ink) and *ancre* (anchor). *Jeter l'encre sur le fond du problème* is a familiar expression meaning "to deliberately obscure a problem." *Jeter l'ancre sur le fond du problème* means the opposite, "to try to come to grips with the problem."

love him"; "I, loving the loving God with love, God will know if I love him." The second pun line may mean: "The loving God, the magnet"; "The magnet God, the loving," or any combination of these. These many possible readings — the final rapprochement with the word "amour," as well as the summarization of all the attributes of the Deity by the one word *aimant* — all these emphasize His loving goodness. The reverse also holds true. The effect implies that if one tries to analyse the meaning of God's love, one can derive from it all his other attributes. Again this creates the impression that the possible meanings of a word are not fortuitous, the result of haphazard phonetic development, but are of fundamental significance, and that the poet, by systematically developing all possible meanings, can explore each word in depth, making it yield its secrets.

When the pun occurs within a comparison, the pun word suggests two comparisons rather than one. Therefore, in "Ici, je suis comme au terrier," (DP, p. 114), which constitutes a *jeu de mots*, *terrier* means either shelter or retreat. A number of similar puns are the focal point of very short (one line) poems:

L'Artillerie du Sacré Cœur, ou la canonisation de Paris.
(CD, p. 59);

Brouillard, étoile d'araignée.
(CD, p. 51).

Canonisation normally has a theological meaning only. In the first example, however, the concise buildup for the pun "l'artillerie du Sacré Cœur" imposes a military analogy, with a twist, since the military meaning is used figuratively. The artillery is divine, as one might speak of the weapons of angels. The second example is somewhat more complex. "Etoile d'araignée" may be characterized as a "portmanteau" phrase, in which two distinct expressions, *toile d'araignée*, meaning "spiderweb," and *étoile*, "star," are welded together to coin a third expression encompassing both the original expressions. The two terms, "brouillard" and "étoile d'araignée," are juxtaposed without any grammatical connectives. The link between the two is a visual analogy which is threefold: The *étoile* and *toile d'araignée* are similar in the general outline of their shape. The juxtaposition of this expression with *brouillard* gives form to the fog. In addition, the fog imparts a blurred quality, a kind of immateriality, to the other two objects, which underlines their gossamer quality. Therefore, any of the objects named becomes a metaphor for the other two. The structure of the comparison, through the elimination of any linking words, achieves great density, and the pun, by superimposing two images within one expression, condenses the imagery still further, while it expands the possible meaning of the comparison.

In the two previous examples, the literal meanings of the pun word suggest the images of the comparison. In other poems, both literal and figurative meanings of the pun word suggest different images. For example, in

>... ... ... ô lune
>car ce soir tu présides du haut de tes tribunes
>à la fête que donne le miroir de l'étang
>   ("Effet de lune," LC, p. 98),

"fête" is the focal point of a metaphorical configuration involving metaphorization both of the moon (personified in "ô lune") and of the lake (though the analogy between the surface of the lake and a mirror). The first appropriate meaning of *fête* which comes to mind is the literal one, "holiday." The reflections of the moon are compared to the lanterns decorating a feast; simultaneously, one would think of dancing and merriment. The image is a double one since "fête" applies equally to the reflections of the moon upon the water, and the reflections of a mirror in the dark. In addition, a special meaning of "fête," as ritual celebration (reinforced by the internal analogy with the ritual of a tribunal) suggests that the nightly appearance of the moon is a rite celebrated by the lake. The figurative associations of *fête:* joy, pomp, sumptuousness, are concretised in the festive metaphor.

Another possibility exists which almost abolishes the distinction between pun and metaphor. This occurs when the pun is based not on multiple existing meanings of a single word but on the symbolic connotations of a word that are almost inseparable from its habitual meaning in contexts of poetry. This is true of archetypal symbols, which immediately bring to mind a wealth of associations. Jacob used this kind of vocabulary quite often, as in the untitled poem in HdC, p. 138:

Ici la neige... Qu'est-ce que ça me fait?
en moi la neige signifie banqueroute.
Guettons, guettez au carrefour des routes
si le printemps ne reviendra jamais.

Each of the several key words, "neige," "route," "printemps," constitutes an archetype, *neige* suggesting either winter (old age) or death; *printemps* rebirth, hope, joy; and *route*, the turning point. In this context, *banqueroute* (normally a business bankruptcy) becomes metaphorical, symbolising failure.

In another poem, allegorical suggestions are superimposed upon archetypal *themes*, of a road not taken, of a magic charm:

...Seigneur, vous m'aviez pourtant fixé un rendez-vous et je ne vais pas... [sic] ... J'avais le droit d'aller au rendez-vous du Sauveur et j'ai perdu la sandale magique. J'avais le devoir d'aller au rendez-vous et j'ai perdu la tunique enchantée...
("Paradis et Enfer," SI, in MC, p. 99).

"Sandale magique," "tunique enchantée," refer to a world of myth in which objects confer magical powers upon their owner, or symbolize certain qualities of the owner — the enchanted tunic being the garment of the elect, the magic sandal symbolizing the ability to pursue the right road. In the context of the poem, the interpretation of the symbols is Christian, since the "rendez-vous du Sauveur" designates, by periphrasis, the appointed day of judgment during which the righteous will be saved. The allegory means that the "lyrical I" mourns the loss of the qualities that would have enabled him to appear at the rendezvous fixed by Christ.

Archetypes produce effects which are considerably more subtle, as in the following poem, entitled "Rebâtissons," in DP, p. 118:

Il suffit qu'un enfant de cinq ans, en sa blouse bleu pâle, dessinât sur un album, pour qu'une porte s'ouvrît dans la lumière, pour que le château se rebâtît, et que l'ocre de la colline se couvrît de fleurs.

On one level, the poem is simply the evocation of a child drawing, with a sketchy suggestion of his drawing — a hill, a castle with a door, and flowers. However, the use of the definite article in front of "château" and "colline" suggests that a particular hill, a particular castle, sally forth at the child's action. This inevitably brings to mind the castles of childhood dreams and hence of legend. "Lumière" is another key word. The door opens into the light. In this context, "light" has more than spiritual connotations: its being followed by "le château" and "la colline" implies that the child's action opens the door directly into another world. This interpretation depends also on the syntax: the use of the passive "Il suffit... pour qu'une porte s'ouvrît... pour que le château se rebâtît... etc." implies that the action of the child sets in motion automatically, and inevitably, the chain of events evoked by the poem. Nothing is stated directly, yet everything in the poem, including the suggestion of color (light blue, ochre), converges to create a magic world of prettiness and freshness, suggestive of purity and innocence. The poem becomes a vision incorporating reality, childhood memories, and symbol.

Paronomasia.

Paronomasia is a structure in which a pun word is repeated. Paronomasia constitutes a more complex and more varied category of puns than puns with a single reference. Repetition of the pun word serves primarily to underline or exploit the differences in meaning inherent in the pun. Generally, however, the repetition itself creates additional effects. A further complicating factor is the different verbal relationships that the term "pun" covers. A pun can be based on differences in meaning of a single word; it can also be based on the rapprochement of homonyms (words alike in sound or spelling but different in meaning) or homophones (words or phrases different in meaning and spelling but similar in sound). The former is called a *jeu de mots;* the latter, a *calembour.* This distinction is irrelevant to the analysis of puns with a single reference since the focus is on the distinctions in meaning created by the use of the pun word. The distinction between *calembour* and *jeu de mots* is relevant to the analysis of paronomasia, however, since the repetition of a pun word contrasting multiple meanings focuses the attention of the reader on sense distinctions, while repetition contrasting homophones focuses the attention of the reader on similarities in sound first, which creates a sound link rather than a sense link. Again, each is discussed separately.

Repetition of a pun word contrasting multiple meanings of the same word.

When a single pun word is repeated, the effects inherent in the contrast of multiple meanings are always present. Repetition of this pun word, however, also results in the creation of a thematic or rhythmic pattern based on the multiple meanings of the pun word. A variety of patterns is possible, depending on the kinds of contrasts involved.

Entirely different meanings of the same word can be contrasted, as in "Angoisses et autres," FddL, n. p.):

> J'ai peur que tu ne t'offenses
> lorsque je mets en balance
> dans mon cœur et dans mes œuvres
> ton amour dont je me prive
> Et l'autre amour dont meurs.
>
> Qu'écriras-tu en ces vers
> ou bien Dieu que tu déranges
> Dieu, les prêtres et les anges
> ou bien tes amours d'enfer
> et leurs agonies gourmandes...

The poet contrasts the love he feels towards his God with a sensual love, evoking the inner conflict this dual allegiance causes him. The allusion to *amours d'enfer,* though veiled, is clearly a reference to the homosexuality of the speaker: the theme is that of Baudelaire's *femmes damnées.* The phrases "dont je meurs" and "agonies," while hyperbolic, are fully justified in a believer. The repetition through successive stanzas of one word, "amour," which expresses the conflicting tendencies of the poet, constitutes a striking way of developing the theme of torment.

Frequently, the repetition of a pun word contrasts a literal with a figurative meaning. The reader progresses from the literal to the figurative or sometimes to the symbolic:

> sous les peupliers où l'on vend les cierges
> où l'on vend les cierges et les comestibles
> c'est ici l'auberge
> des dames sorcières, on y vend les âmes
> > ("Pardon la nuit en Bretagne," HdC, p. 41);
>
> Sur le pas de la porte, la porte des arcs de la Vie
> > ("A propos des rêves: les trois égrégors," DP, p. 9);
>
> Dans l'ennui de mes nuits et la nuit de mes jours
> > ("Nouveau Baptême," HdC, p. 45).

In the first example, the sale becomes progressively more demonic, participating in the atmosphere of superstition and mystery evoked in the poem. The successive repetition of *vend* sharply underlines the transformation of the inn. In the second example, the first door is literal, the second, imaginary and symbolic. The repetition mimics a psychological feeling of hesitation and also underlines the shift in levels of meaning. In the third example, the progression is from real night (antonym of day), to figurative night, anguish, torment. This last is particularly striking because the pun is part of an antithetical conceit, and because the sound *nui* is repeated three times. There is, however, no pun on *ennui,* only a rapprochement of sound.

In a number of instances, a word is repeated in contexts involving what Max Black has called "...a special system [of implications] established for the purpose in hand..."[3] The result is an extension of meaning rather than a contrast between two established meanings. Since both the extended meaning and the usual meaning are contrasted, the device is related both to metaphor and to puns. Consider, as an example, the following poem, entitled "Ver ou serpent," in CD, II, p. 34:

> Ver ou serpent, c'est le démon.
> Les Indiens Peaux Rouges avec des seringues piquent les idoles en bois pourri pour tuer le ver. Puisse Dieu tuer le mien, ce ver solitaire qui me tue...

---

[3] *Models and Metaphors* (Ithaca, 1962), p. 46.

Jacob, starting off with the theme of the snake as tempter, personifying evil, renews the symbol by giving it a highly concrete interpretation: the snake becomes a tapeworm, an interior devil which gnaws, literally and figuratively, at the inside of the person it inhabits.

If the repeated pun word is particularly expressive, particularly rich in lyrical associations, the repetition and successive changes of meaning create a pattern of ever deepening, ever more intense lyrical suggestions. As an example, "ombre" is repeated in the line

> ombre de moi qui fus, reconnais-tu mes ombres

from "La Vraie Jeunesse," DP, p. 38. This line constitutes the leitmotiv of the poem. Throughout the poem, which is a long one, each repetition of "ombre" and of the entire line changes the cognitive meaning of the word — from "different selves," to "shadows of selves," to "ghosts." In addition, each successive meaning evokes a larger context of associated themes — those of death, of the different selves one has been at various times of one's life — so that the word acquires great depth and power of suggestion beyond the clear distinction of multiple meanings normally associated with the pun.

Paronomasia based on repetition of homophones.

The repetition of homophones constitutes an obvious form of punning since the differences in spelling call attention to the differences in meaning. There is no possibility of missing the pun, no subtlety. The very obviousness however makes this pun such an effective structure. It is impossible to miss the point.

The effect of this structure varies with the pattern it assumes. The simplest structures contrast one homophonous word or phrase with another as in

> J'suis entouré! j'suis entouré! j'suis en Touraine
> ("Ecrit pour la S. A. F.," DT, p. 89);

> Il a été témoin d'une scène ou demi-scène de la fille avec la mère à propos de physique ou de fusil, la bonne ayant demandé si on faisait beaucoup de physique ou de fusil...
> ("L'Art ariste," in CD, p. 118).

The result is an attack upon language. In the first example, the repetition of "j'suis entouré" ("I am surrounded") sets up a potentially dramatic situation. With "J'suis en Touraine," however, the poem abruptly changes direction. This phrase, by imitating and distorting the dramatic lines, and by substituting a second meaning totally inappropriate to the dramatic situation, abruptly deflates it: the tension is dissolved with a burst of laughter. In the second example, *demi-scène* is a coined word. The repetition of *scène*, prefixed by *demi, as* well as that of the homophones *physique* and *fusil*, successively proposes different readings, so that the story refuses to be told; the words cease to communicate. In each of these examples, a meaning is simultaneously set up and destroyed, so that the structure functions as a metalinguistic commentary which erodes the cognitive content of the message.

Where a series of homophonous phrases rather than words are juxtaposed, the structure is more complex since the sound link is apparent before the sense link. This is particularly striking when associated with a pattern of repetition that is frequent in Jacob's poetry: the juxtaposition of homophones without grammatical connectives of any sort. These can be homophonous phrases:

> Mes grelots, maigre lot...
> (Untitled, VI, p. 27);

> Sa crédence sacrée danse.
> ("Déménagement de la sacristie," DP, p. 139);

> Terrasses et toits, terrasse-toi, terre assez: toi.
> ("Métaphysique," SI, in MC, p. 98).

or even occasionally, entire homophonous sentences:

> J'ai un mari honnête, je suis maligne, honnête et pourtant je ne suis qu'une marionnette.
> (Untitled, CD, I, p. 238);

> La bourse houle! avis!
> La bourse ou la vie
> La bout sous la vie

(Glas! boue!) sourd, l'ami
Glabre, ours sous l'habit.
("Variation d'une formule," SM, p. 229).

In these series, the homophones are given as interchangeable in that they are pronounced almost exactly alike. If the poem were heard rather than read, the similarity of sound would make it appear that the entire poem consisted of a repetition of the same word or phrase. As a result, it would be incomprehensible. When the poem is read, however, only the suggestion of incomprehensibility is retained, but the impression of the interchangeability of the sounds is added. This could appear to be a game, a way of juggling sounds in a contrived and artificial manner to obtain the maximum number of possible variations. This kind of juxtaposition of approximate sounds, however, creates surprising relationships of meaning since interchangeability of sound becomes associated with interchangeability of meaning. Moreover, each successive homophonous series results in a change of meaning which is entirely unexpected but completely apt. Each homophone, therefore, appears to be an interpretation in depth of the preceding one. For example, in "J'ai un mari honnête..." (which constitutes an entire poem), each homophonous phrase gives a cruel interpretation of the one preceding it; each one reveals a meaning opposite to the one which the speaker intended, each one more pejorative and satirical than the one before it. The impression is left that the meaning of a word can turn treacherously against itself. And the poem, a monologue placed in the mouth of a *bourgeoise*, becomes a moral and philosophical caricature of its subject by herself. The homophonous series beginning with "Terrasses et toits..." occurs immediately after the phrase: "existence du non-moi." The context is lyrical, but the result is similar. An image which is primarily visual, "terrasses et toits," becomes, through successive interpretations, an admonition to humility "terrasse-toi," "humble yourself," and a phrase juxtaposing both the futility of earthly existence ("terre assez"), and the choice of Christ or the Deity ("toi"). The last segment may be translated as "earth enough: you." In this series, an additional effect is that the first image, that of "terraces and roofs," retrospectively acquires metaphoric overtones: of graves or terraces above the earth. As in the previous example, however, the main thrust of the homophonous series is that the successive modifications each phrase undergoes constitute an exploration in depth of the meaning of the phrase on a philosophical level, an interpretation reinforced, in this instance, by the title of the poem "Métaphysique." Ultimately, the implication of such a sound/sense sequence is that by seeking out all the possible meaningful sound combinations of words, the poet uncovers their essential meaning.

Repeated homophones, like other types of puns, can be associated with metaphor or can play other, varying structural roles in the poem. The tendency with homophones, however, is towards incongruity, towards intensification of surprise effects. This can be shown by analysis of the often-quoted:

> Comme un bateau, le poète est âgé
> Ainsi qu'un dahlia, le poème étagé
> Dahlia! Dahlia! que Dalila lia.
>
> (Untitled, LC, p. 101).

This metaphor contains a number of sound links: the homophones *est âgé* and *étagé* at the rhyme; the repetition of *dahlia,* and the homophonous approximation between *dahlia* and *Dalila,* echoed in *lia*. Similarly, there are a number of analogies: the comparison between the flower and the poem suggests an analogy between the image of the flower and the internal structure of the poem; and the final *que Dalila lia* suggests a complex metaphor in that the bouquet tied by Dalila can be either a visual bouquet (of dahlias or Samson's hair), or the bouquet of the poem, whose unity resides in the sound links suggested by the noun Dalila and the analogy of the dahlia. No real connection exists between the first and second lines of the image except for the *rime riche* of the homophones. The image is precious and contrived, yet striking because of the homophones.

Repeated homophones in a title create surprise effects, whether the title contains a pun, developed by the rest of the poem, or whether the body of the poem constitutes the build-up for a pun. One example is the poem in CD, p. 120, entitled "Sir Élizabeth (prononcez soeur)." The parenthesis in the title initially appears to contain a phonetic indication, necessary for the French reader unacquainted with English pronunciation. The pun "sir/soeur" is therefore bilingual. Curiosity is aroused, however, by the incongruous association between Sir, a male title, and Élizabeth, a feminine name. This is justified in the poem by an amusing anecdote which motivates the antithesis of the title: it is revealed that "Sir Élizabeth" is indeed a woman, called "Sir" because she became a soldier when scorned by her lover.

An even more incongruous effect is created by certain poems which, like the preceding, appear initially to be developed around puns, and yet, once the poem has been read, leave the feeling that the significance of the homophonic pun must be sought elsewhere than in this structure. One such poem is "Le Sacrifice d'Abraham," CD, p. 141:

> En temps de famine en Irlande, un amoureux disait avec ardeur à une veuve: "Une escalope de vô, ma divine! —Non! dit la veuve, je ne voudrais pas abîmer ce corps que vous me faites la grâce d'admirer! Mais elle fit venir son enfant et lui coupa un beau morceau saignant à l'endroit de l'escalope. Est-ce que l'enfant garda la cicatrice? Je ne sais pas; il hurlait bibliquement quand on le coupa dans l'escalope.

The poem develops a homophonic pun: *escalope de vô*, a misquotation of *escalope de veau*, translatable either as "veal cutlet" or "a cutlet out of you." The second meaning is the one developed. In addition, the poem fuses two literary sources: Swift's *Modest Proposal* and the Biblical story of Abraham's sacrifice. The style is the deadpan, serious style of Swift. (Note "et lui coupa un beau morceau saignant" — and she cut him a nice juicy slice" — which is the way one would speak about a veal cutlet rather than a human cutlet). The structural pattern, the successive interpretation of puns through homophonous approximation, places the focus of the poem on "bibliquement," so that "il hurlait bibliquement" takes on the meaning of "he screamed like a Banshee." It is not satisfactory, however, to think of this poem primarily as a witticism. Too many other suggestions nag the reader. The allusion to Swift suggests that the poem is either a parody or an imitation of his work. The title also hints at a satirical intention. Or the poem can be considered an example of "humour noir," a "sick" joke. None of these possibiilties can be eliminated, and a precise meaning cannot be assigned to this apparently simple text. Yet the reader, precisely because of its simplicity, is unable to merely shrug off the poem. He feels he ought to understand it. And so it remains, nagging, simple — and obscure, its obscurity primarily the result of the fact that the reader wishes to interpret a poem which resists interpretation.

One poem, leading up to a pun, is puzzling, apparently not because it is ambiguous, but because it would seem to be a *poème manqué:*

> J'ai revu mon ancien professeur de rhétorique et avec une femme. Je n'ai vu que leurs têtes mangeant des éclairs au chocolat sans plaisir: la grosse tête de l'ennui et la petite tête du commandement. Ah! Ah! la revanche de l'humanité sur les humanités. Or, je me suis retenu d'aller par vengeance: c'est ici la revanche des humanités sur l'humanité.
> (Untitled, CD, p. 61).

Evidently, the desire to end the poem with a paradox led Jacob to invert the first "la revanche de l'humanité sur les humanités" in the concluding sentence. Yet the poem does not make sense unless the concluding sentence reads "c'est ici la revanche de l'humanité sur les humanités."

Sound links.

Sound links are more difficult to define than the various types of puns. My analysis of puns was based on clearly defined, generally accepted semantic distinctions and/or patterns. Such clearly delimited criteria do not exist for sound links. Broadly speaking, any type of verbal association or sequence that seems to be dominated by the patterns of the sounds themselves can be considered as a species of sound link. This category is potentially very broad since it could include onomatopoeia, alliteration, rhyme, or rhythmical effects. I will consider, however, only such associations of words as would elicit the judgments "nonsense," "doggerel," "mere playful exercise," "automatism," or the like, yet would impress the reader first by their sound patterns.

Sound links are related to homophones. The differences between the two, however, are clear, despite some overlap. Although the homophones considered were a sub-species of the pun, sound links need not result in a pun effect. More importantly, sound links are not restricted to any structural pattern. The potential patterns available to the writer are limited only by his ingenuity. They can be limited to deformations of individual words, or extend over sentences, or entire poems; follow predictable sequences, or be totally unpredictable. No other form of verbal play gives the writer such freedom to juggle language and meaning, and it is this freedom which makes the use of sound links so striking, and so controversial.

Patterns of sound association which deform individual words are so close in effect to the homophonous use of puns, that they could be considered a sub-species of homophones. The structural variety exhibited by this group, however, reflects the penchant towards gratuity, towards whimsy, which is characteristic of sound links. The varieties of individual word deformations in Jacob's work are numerous. He sometimes divides a word, as in

> Prends les ossements de quiconque:
> Ce tibia a forme de quille
> Et ce crâne a forme de conque.
> ("La Mort, II," HdC, p. 161).

where the first syllable of *quille* suggests to Jacob its homophones *qui* and *quille;* the second, the homonym *conque*. This constitutes a kind of etymological punning, with the twist that, in this instance, the images, based on homophony, are totally unexpected since they derive from an unnatural division of the deformed word, *quiconque*. Part of a word in a similar manner, is broken off, to form another one which defines the first:

> Le brazéro, zéro! ...
> (Untitled, CD, p. 64).

Syllables are also added to words or subtracted from them:

> On appelle homme-cygnes ou hommes insignes les hommes qui ont le cou long, comme Fénelon, cygne de Cambrai.
>
> ("Le Cygne [genre essai plein d'esprit]," CD, p. 91).

In this last example, the etymological punning and verbal deformation lead around to the final pun in a perfect circle which returns to the original meaning of the term. The "hiccup" effect, also a species of etymological punnings, results from the repetition of one syllable:

> ...au taureau haut qui n'est qu'un homme et qui combat, bas!
>
> ("Equatoriales solitaires," CD, p. 152),

Finally words transform themselves into others: by changing part of the word, as in the title:

> Paralysie — parasitisme.
>
> (CD, p. 81);

by consonant changes, as in another title:

> Capitale: tapis de table.
>
> (CD, p. 144);

by the addition of extra syllables:

> J'suis le bouquet
> J'suis le bouquet
> J'suis le bouc émissaire,[4]

or by progressive interversion of sounds:

> Les manèges déménagent
>
> Manèges, ménageries, où?... et pour quels voyages?
>
> Moi qui suis en ménage
> Depuis... ah! y a bel âge!

---

[4] Quoted by Jean Rousselot, in *Max Jacob au sérieux*, p. 170.

> De vous goûter, manèges,
> Je n'ai plus... que n'ai-je...?
>   L'âge.
>   ("Avenue du Maine," SM, p. 229).

The effect of these word transformations is similar to the rapprochement between sound and sense noted in juxtaposed homophonous series, or indeed any species of popular etymologies. The impression created is that sound and sense are related, that by playing with sound, by seeking out all the possible meanings of various sound combinations of one word or phrase, the poet is revealing unsuspected layers of reality.

Patterns of sound association that extend over lengthy verbal sequences constitute the structure most characteristic of sound links. Such sequences can take a number of forms. Words can be grouped by an extension of the principle of homophony, echoing, for example, syllable sounds rather than approximating the entire word:

> Cet Allemand était fou d'art, de foulards, de poulardes.
>   (Untitled, CD, p. 69).

They can be grouped on the basis of similar radicals:

> ...il est traversé de rails bleus qui se rallient, le raient et le raillent.
>   (Untitled, CD, p. 64).

Or dissimilar sound sequences can follow one another in various series:

> Le toit, c'est quatre, quatre, quatre: il y en a quatre. Le perron est une pelouse que nous opérons et qui les jalouse. Les toits sont amarante: reflet d'orage! rage! rage! et l'ensemble est en sucre, en stuc, en ruche, moche, riche.
>   (Untitled, CD, p. 63).

These patterns are illustrative only. Others are possible. They are of importance not so much in themselves, but because they leave the impression that the texts in which they appear were derived in an "automatic" manner, that the genesis of the poem can be followed through an evolution based on a pattern of association of sounds, or in poems other than those cited, of ideas; and finally, that the pattern of association renders the poem intelligible, is, in fact, the key to its interpretation. Poems based on association of sound have been interpreted in this manner by Suzanne Bernard and Yvon Belaval.[5] The genesis of a poem, however, usually is not known to the reader. Even when it is known, moreover, it does not necessarily explain the poem. In the case of poems seemingly based on sound links, the sound patterns are misleading in that they only make it appear that the poem is logically structured. In reality, these poems can be interpreted in many ways, and a broad spectrum of possibilities exists for interpretation, from clarity, through fantasy, to non-communication.

At one pole, that of clarity, the pattern of sound association structures the poem especially when the sound pattern is associated with imagery. The result is primarily rhythmic, but the rhythm appears dissonant, or choppy. The poem, however, remains interpretable. One example is:

> Le brazéro, zéro! il s'exaspère de n'être pas un triangle muni d'ailes noires. Il se mord la queue, il est traversé de rails bleus qui se rallient, le raient, et le raillent.
>
> (Untitled, CD, p. 64).

A *brazéro* is a brazier, a pan for holding live coals. The homophonous series (or approximations) of "Il est traversé de rails bleus qui se rallient, le raient et le raillent" are based on similar radicals. This can, as in earlier examples, create the impression of a possible link between sound and sense. Primarily, however, this homophonic grouping constitutes a dynamic yet very concrete evocation of the *brazéro*, personified humorously as a self-devouring soul, aspiring to be something other than he is: he is shaped like a triangle, but would like to be a triangle "muni d'ailes noires." The homophonous series give expression to his "torment." Moreover, the pun in "raient" means both that the rails which

---

[5] See Suzanne Bernard, *Le Poème en prose de Baudelaire jusqu'à nos jours*, p. 632; and Yvon Belaval, *La Rencontre avec Max Jacob* (Paris, 1946), pp. 93-96.

constitute the *brazéro* "stripe" him and "obliterate" him; there is also a pun based on a rapprochement of the homonyms "rails" (rails), and "raillent" (which means "to mock"). This link between *rails* and *raillent* repeats the initial etymological link between *brazéro* and *zéro*: the source of the brazéro's torment lies both in his definition of himself, and in the fact that the very physical elements which constitute his make-up (the rails) mock and obliterate him.

Somewhat more difficult to interpret, more ambiguous; is the following (again, an entire poem), untitled, from CD, p. 65:

> Ma Séléné à moi n'est pas la vaseline énorme avec,
> O Séléné, du démêlé, du démêloir, tout autour, c'est rayé
> de jaune, de l'onyx qui brûle et brille.

There are two patterns of sound associations: the first based on the repetition of *élé* in *Séléné*, *démêlé*, and *démêloir*; the second on the juxtaposition of the two homophones *brûle* and *brille*. The numerous difficulties in this poem stem more from the vocabulary than from the repetition of sounds. *Démêlé* may be interpreted either as an adjective or as a noun. As a noun, it would mean "quarrel," which is inappropriate in this context. Its meaning as an adjective, "disentangled," must therefore be the one intended. The use of the partitive in front of it turns it into a concrete noun. A *démêloir* is a large comb. Normally, a partitive designates part of a quantity in a noun in the singular. Its use in front of a noun such as comb transforms its meaning, but not in a precise way. The analogy between the moon and *vaseline* is a very bold one. The assimilation of a mythological deity (Séléné) and a most commonplace object is so shocking that the visual comparison between the moon and the cross section of a jar of vaseline is not immediately obvious. "Séléné" is both the moon (visual image) and goddess of love, protectress of women. With the contrast between the soft (vaseline) and the hard (onyx), the poem becomes clear. It contrasts two different visions of the moon. The first section evokes an image of the moon, both visual and tactile, associated with its soft, feminine character, by suggesting objects or characteristics of a lady's boudoir: comb, pommade, etc. The second contrasts this image of the moon with the poet's personal vision of it: "onyx striped with yellow which burns and shines," an image of great visual intensity, almost hallucinatory. The contrasts between the soft and hard suggest discreetly a further contrast between two different types of eroticism associated with each vision of the moon. The choppy rhythm resulting from the division of phrases into very short fragments and the dissonant sounds created by the repetition of homophones are entirely appropriate because they underline the disturbing character of the poet's personal vision of the moon (and perhaps the erotic overtones of the poem as well). A number of familiar objects are made to appear totally new, through the rhythm created by the associations of sounds, the incongruity of the objects evoked, and the symbolic overtones they acquire.

In a related example:

> Le toit, c'est quatre, quatre, quatre: il y en a quatre. Le perron est une pelouse que nous opérons et qui les jalouse. Les toits sont amarante: reflet d'orage! rage! rage! et l'ensemble est un sucre, en stuc, en ruche, moche, riche.
>
> (Untitled, CD, p. 63),

one homophonic series proceeds into the next. No logical transition exists between them. The first sentence: "Le toit, c'est quatre, quatre,..." is entirely meaningless as a cognitive statement, as a definition of the roof. The repetition of *quatre*, however, mimics the repetition of a succession of rooftops. The words of the second section "rage," "moche," (a slang word meaning ugly), "jalouse" suggest ugly and angry emotions. The choppy rhythm created by the exclamations and the breakdown of the sentences into short phrases or single words underlines these affective connotations by suggesting the tone and the gestures of anger. What emerges is not so much a visual image, as a dynamic complex of emotions about a particular landscape.

In other poems, obscurity intensifies as the context imposes various types of ambiguity. One example is the following untitled poem, from CD, p. 69, quoted here in its entirety:

> Cet Allemand était fou d'art, de foulards et de poulardes. Dans son pays, la reine-Claude est peinte sur les

foulards; à table, on en sait aussi qui rôdent autout des poulardes.

In this case, the homophonous series in the first sentence constitute an approximation rather than an exact equivalent. Writing *reine-Claude* without a capital results in a pun since *reine-Claude* indicates either the fruit (a plum), or "queen Claude." At first the poem appears to be one whose homophones play a structural role and are developed further by the poem. Yet this appearance of organization is deceptive. The poem neither begins nor ends; the details supplied have no readily identifiable significance: who is this "Allemand?" *Cet,* the demonstrative adjective, normally precedes a noun whose antecedent is known, but this is clearly not the case. Is the additional information meant to reflect on the bad taste of the Germans, who paint plums or queens on scarves? Or is the entire poem a parody of a kind of inane table conversation? No one interpretation either fits entirely or excludes any other.

This type of poem is made up of coherent sentences, which follow each other logically. It is internally consistent. Yet ultimately, no meaning can be assigned to it. And this produces a kind of frustration which is all the more strong because the text is apparently so simple.

Other texts are simultaneously more obscure and more evocative. Consider, as an example, the following very brief untitled poem, from CD, p. 55:

> L'enfant, l'éfant, l'éléphant, la grenouille et la pomme sautée.

It is proof of the compelling nature of this text that another author, Yvon Belaval,[6] also singled it out for extensive analysis. My own analysis had been written when I came across his; they overlap only partially. The poem presents a number of difficulties. Some of them are semantic. "Efant" appears to be entirely an imaginary word, invented by Jacob. Belaval notes in a footnote of his analysis that he had also considered *éfant* an invented word,

---

[6] See *La Recherche de la poésie* (Paris, 1947), pp. 38-43.

until Mssrs. Queneau and Paulhan informed him that *éfant* was the usual way of referring to a child in the patois of Lower Normandy. There is no way of knowing whether Jacob was aware of this. More importantly, the reader, even if he is a very cultured Frenchman, is unlikely to know an obscure patois word, and would, as Belaval initially did, consider the word imaginary. The context, furthermore, gives no clue as to its possible meaning. The phrase "la pomme sautée" is equally troublesome. *Pomme sautée*, in French, ordinarily instantly brings to mind a common variety of fried potatoes. Belaval rejects this particular meaning as too vulgar or pedestrian, but in so doing, he is simply considering ordinary reality "anti-poetic." *Sautée* can have two other meanings, however: jumped ("the apple which was jumped," possibly by a leaping frog), or skipped, omitted ("the apple which was omitted, which did not occur"). (*Pomme sautée* could not mean the jumping apple which would be *la pomme sautant*). Since the context does not give any clues, any of these meanings are legitimate. These obscurities are compounded by the fact that all the nouns are preceded by the definite article, which ordinarily implies allusions to familiar objects which the reader would instantly recognize. But the absence of any obvious reference compels the reader to consider a wide variety of possible contexts — literary, historical, biblical or the like, in which the objects enumerated would be associated in a logical fashion. The nature of the enumeration, however, condemns these efforts to frustration.

The poem juxtaposes, without connectives of any sort, a collection of objects. The first three "L'enfant, l'éfant, l'éléphant," seem to be grouped on the basis of homophonic association. The final two objects in the series, the "grenouille" and the "pomme sautée" do not fit this scheme, however which leads to conjecture about how the two series came to be associated in the mind of the poet. The frog, which is thought of as a jumping animal, might have suggested the image of *sauter*, which was then transferred to the apple. There seems to be no other connection between the first and second sections of the poem. More importantly, the association of ideas which presided over the genesis of the poem does not in itself give any clue to the significance of the enumeration. It could designate a collection of heterogeneous objects; or it could be an ordered series. The predisposition to seek order and logic leads to an attempt at a logical interpretation of the text. But its lack of internal clarity will resist such attempts. Ultimately, such a text triggers a series of associations and fantasies. A number of interpretations can be invented, none excluding the others. I offer the following as illustrations of how this game might work.

Try to pinpoint the allusion to the apple (or potato). The first one to occur to me is the Biblical apple. "Sautée" in this context logically means "skipped," meaning that the apple had never existed, or never been bitten. Either way, I am projected back into a state of innocence. The rest of the poem can easily be fitted into this interpretation. The "enfant," the "éléphant" and the "grenouille" constitute a heterogeneous collection of innocent beings, assembled harmoniously in this mythological state, much as they might be assembled in a primitive painting. The "éfant," because of all the associations which this context evokes, becomes a being who has disappeared from our world, a symbol of lost innocence. Jacob's aphorism (in *Art Poétique*, p. 73, my translation): "I dreamt of recreating the life of this earth in the atmosphere of heaven" would serve as a perfect epigraph for this interpretation. This interpretation, moreover, even accomodates the pedestrian fried potato. The meanings of "la pomme sautée" as the "omitted apple" and the fried potato can both fit. Fried potatoes bring to mind cooking, domesticity, utility, evoking an order of nature in which domesticity and innocence co-exist. The poem then becomes an evocation of a mythological state of nature such as Jean Jacques Rousseau might have dreamt, where civilization has not brought about corruption.

If the poem is thought of as enumerating an ordered series, a number of possibilities exist: one, as a progression from a higher to a lower form of life, a retrogression; or perhaps, a parody of poems linking sound and sense, tracing evolution from the child (man), though an imaginary being (the *éfant*), through the animal kingdom (the *éléphant* and the *grenouille*), finally through the apple, as Brisset had established through analysis of words that man is descended from the frog. We could also interpret *sautée* as jumped, the apple over which something (perhaps the frog) jumped. This introduces a touch of action, of dynamism. The poem then becomes the evocation of an idyllic, animated state of nature.

Evidently, each reader will bring to such a poem his own experience, and this, as well as the nature of the text, will affect the associations the poem will evoke. To Belaval, for example, the rhythm of the poem is reminiscent both of recitations French children perform in school, and of children's songs, for example: "Un éléphant, Ça trompe, ça trompe / Un éléphant / Ça trompe les enfants," in which one finds both *enfant* and *éléphant;* or "Pomme de reinette et pomme d'api, / Tapis, tapis rouge..." Enough has been said to establish that so many possibilities for suggestion exist only because of the ambiguities in the poem. The order and logic suggested by the use of the definite article are important, not because they mean that the poem is in fact logical, but because they *imply* that it is. And this appearance of logic combined with the obscurities locked into the poem compels fantasy and the appeal to the imagination.

In some poems, however, communication almost ceases:

> Boum! Dame! Amsterdam!
> Barège n'est pas Baume-les-Dames!
> Papa n'est pas là!
> L'ipéca du rat n'est pas du chocolat.
> Gros lot du Congo? oh! le beau Limpopo!
> Port du mort, il sort de l'or *(bis)*.
> Clair de mer de verre de terre
> Rage, mage, déménage
> Du fromage où tu nages
> Papa n'est pas là.
> L'ipéca du Maradjah de Nepala.
> Pipi, j'ai envie
> Hi! faut y l'dire ici.
> Vrai? Vrai?
> ("Musique acidulée," LC, p. 169).

The poem consists of a series of phrases each of which could be excerpted from a child's speech, including word games such as *contrepéteries* (phrases in which various letters are interverted so that a new meaning emerges): "clair de mer de verre de terre;" associations through rhyme: "rage, mage, déménage / Du fromage où tu nages;" and snatches of conversation: "Papa n'est pas là," many of which show delight in scatology: "Pipi, j'ai envie / Hi! faut y l'dire ici." In the first two lines, an onomatopoeic and rhythmic element evokes the sonority and rhythm of a children's marching song. The entire poem evokes memories of one's childhood, and of similar word games, expressions, or songs. Yet beyond that, communication ends. Many sentences are internally inconsistent, or meaningless in cognitive terms. They do not form any predictable or analysable sequence, but are strung along at random. The title underlines the rhythmic elements of the poem, and its over-all jarring effect, but does not provide any other clues. The poem can be assembled and disassembled in any fashion until the conclusion is reached that the poem is cognitively meaningless, that no ingeniousness will ever make it mean anything more than what is stated "Boum! Dame! Amsterdam!" and that indeed, the only intention that can be ascribed to such a poem, and to the poet who wrote it, is that it was meant to systematically resist any attempt to be interpreted. The result is a paradox since language is deliberately used, not for purposes of communication, but to create a hermetic object with limited communication potential. This is not perverse or bad; it simply represents another way of calling into question the reader's assumptions about language, analogous to some surrealist experiments.

Earlier in the chapter, we enumerated the ways in which the use of puns extends the expressive possibilities of poetry. We have traveled full circle, analysing many possibilities until reaching that of non-communication. The poetic ends, however, are the same in all cases; as Jacob stated them in the preface to *Le Cornet à dés*, to "transplant" the reader; that is, to project him into a universe whose logic and appearance are unlike his own. Sound and word play serve these ends since familiar words, suddenly strangers, become the instrument whereby the reader renews his perceptions and assumptions concerning language and reality.

CHAPTER II

THE CLICHE IN PARODY

While certain border-line cases are difficult to distinguish, the terms pastiche and parody are not synonymous. A pastiche is an imitation, an attempt to reproduce a model exactly. A parody, however, distorts and thereby transforms in some way the element it parodies.[1] A true pastiche is relatively rare: most often, it is only an exercise, although it can also be a testimonial of one's admiration. Two types of parody exist. Generally, parody is associated with satire and humor. It can also, however, through imitation and distortion, serve as the starting point for a work which, although it contains elements identifying it with a model, has sufficient autonomy so that it does not seem merely an imitation of the original. In music, such "parodying" has always been an important source of development: one thinks, for example, of Bartok or Stravinsky's borrowing of folk themes.[2] Similarly, there are many literary examples of creative parody: *Don Quijote* is probably the most famous.

True pastiches are infrequent in Jacob's poetry — with the exception of isolated lines recalling other poets which are probably instances of involuntary imitations.[3] Parodies, however, abound.

---

[1] For a fuller discussion of parody and pastiche, see the issue of *CAIEF* devoted to that subject, XI (June 1947).
[2] See Robert Siohan, "Les Formes musicales de la parodie et du pastiche," *CAIEF, op. cit.*, 75-90.
[3] Jacob's Breton poems constitute another important exception. These consist of poems published in 1911 in *La Côte*; and of others, written under the pseudonym of Morven le Gaelique, assembled in one volume *Poèmes de Morven le Gaelique,* published posthumously in 1953. They were an attempt

Many of them are as can be expected — satirical or ironic. Many, especially among prose poems, are far too complex to be considered in such narrow terms, however. The poetic significance of these is difficult to grasp, especially since they parody genres not only outside the traditional conventions of poetry (such as novels), but outside the traditional boundaries of literature (in cluding, for example, *romans feuilletons*, newspaper style, or even recipes).

It is impossible to draw absolute distinctions between "creative" and "satirical" parodies. In some instances, it cannot be stated where a distortion ceases to be satirical or ironic and acquires a different function; in fact, it can be both: *Don Quijote* is at once a parody of *novelas de caballeria* and one of the world's great novels, having created two unforgettable literary types. The analysis of parodies, unlike that of other stylistic devices requires reference to a context outside the immediate literary context. Whether a poem is perceived as a satirical or a creative parody depends however, not on its model, but on the immediate context. A satirical parody aims its shafts at a specific target, the model for the parody. The distortions in the poem clearly render the model ridiculous, so that only one interpretation is possible, and that is satirical. Creative parodies, on the other hand, are more complex. Satirical elements do not necessarily dominate the poem, which can be interpreted in a number of ways. Characteristically, the reader is left with a feeling of disorientation which stems from the poem's resistance to simple interpretations.

The basic literary structure operative in parody is a particular form of the cliché. Ordinarily, the cliché is a structure which is easily identifiable: to use Riffaterre's definition, it is a group of words which elicits judgments such as "*déja vu*, banal, hackneyed, false elegance, worn out, fossilized, why not just talk like everyone else, etc." [4] The cliche functions as one word: the entire group is recognized as a sterotyped structure or a little

---

to transcribe into modern French the folkloric themes of Jacob's native Brittany. See Hélène Henry, "Max Jacob et la Bretagne," *Europe*, No. 348-49 (April May 1958), 7-18.

[4] Michael Riffaterre, "Fonction du cliché dans la prose littéraire," *CAIEF*, XVI (March 1964), 82.

quotation. This definition is not suitable for analysis of the role of the cliché in parody, for what is often involved here is not an exact quote. The cliché in parody designates any feature of style — whether a particular rhetorical figure, a specific turn of syntax, a specific vocabulary, or even something as diffuse as a theme, or a combination of all of these — which is thought to be characteristic of any author, genre, or school, for example, Hugo's use of antithesis, such words as *"ombre," "terrible,"* the use of periphrasis in classical or neo-classical poetry, etc. Generally, such clichés appear in groups. We can distinguish further between two categories of cliché: those which reproduce syntactical or rhetorical devices associated with their model (structural clichés), and clichés which recall their model on a more abstract level, through similarities in theme, vocabulary, etc.

The analysis of the parodic function of the cliché is analogous to that of the stylistic device knows as "renewal" of the cliché. With this device, the expressive potential is restored by altering the cliché structurally: words are added or subtracted, or some of its grammatical components are changed. The starting point, however, must remain identifiable: without recognition of the cliché, there can be no renewal of it. Similarly, in parody, elements of style, theme, or vocabulary must remain identifiable with a tradition which is not that of the author under consideration: there can be no parody without recognition of a model.

Ironical or Satirical Parody

In Jacob's poetry a parody can be spotted by its title. The principle involved is twofold: irony — stating the opposite of what is really meant — and comical exaggeration. Any poem entitled "vrai" or "véritable poème," (a common title, especially in CD), is generally satirical. In contrast, many poems are called simply *Poème*. The implication is that the poem speaks for itself. If the reader is reassured by the adjective *vrai* or *véritable* that he is reading a poem, the chances are that he is reading a parody of one. There are variations of this title. For example, a section of the "Pièces burlesques" in SM, p. 218, is called "Quelques chants vraiment nationaux." When an entire school, genre, or style is the target of satire rather than a particular author, the title embodies the particular features of style which are being satirized. "Vie et marée," in CD, p. 183, precedes a poem parodying romantic lyric poetry. The facile, broad symbolism inherent in the juxtaposition of "life" and the "tides of the sea," in a volume of poetry as far from traditional lyricism as is *Le Cornet à dés*, immediately puts the reader on guard. Similarly, the length of the title: "Le Citadin mort à l'amour de la nature lui adresse ses adieux" (LC, p. 74), its pompousness, again in contrast to the rest of the book, surprises the reader. The length of the title is a warning that the poem falls outside the esthetic values of the twentieth century. The conjunction of themes, poetic diction, and vocabulary reveals the model which is the target of the parody. The themes, "amour de la nature," farewells to the countryside," abound in neo-classical poetry. "Citadin," "amour de la nature," recall the vocabulary of eighteenth century neo-classicism, as does the poetic diction of "adieux." The "involuntary" ambiguity (given as an example of bad writing) in "le citadin mort," leaves the impression for a moment that a dead city dweller is about to speak, and then there is the inappropriateness of addressing one's farewells to the countryside when one no longer loves it. Therefore, the length of the title, its archaic themes, as well as the ineptness of its phrasing, all these make it seem gauche, pompous, and funny. Other comical effects are also possible. A parodic ballad is entitled: "Traduit de l'Allemand ou du Bosniaque." (CD, p. 77). "Traduit de l'Allemand..." would imply an "*A la manière de*..."; that is, a pastiche. The "ou," however, suggests that there is no real model, that the first part of the title is a jest. It serves as an indication that what follows is nonsense. Moreover, "Bosnia," to a Frenchman, connotes a foreign principality, small, quaint, and provincial. The notion that anything might be translated from the "Bosniaque" would immediately appear humorous to him. The juxtaposition of "Allemand" and "Bosniaque" deflates Germany since it is brought down to the level of Bosnia.

Occasionally, the title of a parodic poem departs from these models by warning that the poem is one which ordinarily would not be to the author's taste. A number of poems are entitled: "Poème dans un goût qui n'est pas le mien." (CD, p. 29 and p. 30, for example.) One of these bears the epigraph: "A toi, Rimbaud," revealing the model. Another is entitled "Poème du Java de M. René Ghil et s'appelant les Ksours." (CD, p. 72.) "Poème déclamatoire" CD, p. 36, is in fact a declamatory poem.

The line "... oh! les verts caoutchoucs d'une cour de collège" (Deux Exercices d'exotisme," SM, p. 233) is a good example of satirical parody. This phrase suggests two models. Its syntax duplicates exactly one of Baudelaire's most quoted lines: "Mais le vert paradis des amours enfantines." The similarity is reinforced by the appearance of the adjective *vert* in both formulae. Jacob's phrase is also reminiscent of the kind of exclamation frequently found in Rimbaud's poetry: "Oh" followed by an evocation of something lost and deeply regretted such as "Oh! les pierres précieuses qui se cachaient..."[5] or "O la face cendrée, l'écusson de crin."[6] Again, the syntax is identical: a substantive followed by an adjectival phrase. Jacob, however, parodies the theme of evoking something deeply regretted by substituting for it an object, "green raincoats" whose connotations are certainly utilitarian and perhaps unpleasant. In addition, whereas in the Baudelaire or Rimbaud formulae the adjectival phrases further reinforce the fond associations evoked by the object named, the connotations of the adjectival phrase in Jacob's formula, "d'une cour de collège," reinforce the generally unpleasant character of "green raincoats." Finally, in the Baudelaire phrase, *vert* contributes to the overall effect by connoting both freshness and color; again, in the Jacob phrase, the *vert* is heavily literal. The connotations suggested by Jacob's line strike the reader as ludicrous; the surprise is comic. In a Baudelaire or Rimbaud poem, the connotations are lyrical, as is the surprise. The reaction to Jacob's text, laughter, mocks the object evoked and, beyond it, through a recognition of its models, the lyrical rhetoric which it recalls.

The structure of the preceding example combines structural clichés and thematic elements that recall a model with internal elements that deflate the model by substituting humorous themes in lieu of those evoked. This pattern can dominate an entire

---

[5] Arthur Rimbaud, "Après le déluge," *Œuvres complètes* (Paris, 1954), p. 176.

[6] *Ibid*, "Being Beauteous," p. 181.

poem. Thus, "le Citadin mort à l'amour de la nature lui adresse ses adieux" (LC, p. 73) suggests its model chiefly through an accumulation of ornamental rhetorical figures such as periphrases:

> Forêts, vastes herbiers d'un divin herboriste
> urne, humble trophée
> Roi de l'oubli

or *épithètes de nature:*

> agreste concours
> sombres eaux du Styx
> glacial exil

as well as through a highly stylized conventional setting — in a countryside containing urns, shepherds, grottoes, ruins at sunset, references to Greek deities and the muses — all of which are characteristic of neo-classical poetry. The theme of the poem is ostensibly a serious and philosophical one: the meditations of a "citadin" who while contemplating "nature," has intimations of his own mortality. The reader is prevented from taking this theme seriously first of all because its treatment (through an accumulation of devices and references so alien to the twentieth century) identifies it with an obsolete esthetic tradition. Other characteristics of style further deflate the theme. All the figures cited, except for the first reference, are clichés of neo-classical style. This accumulation of clichés is particularly obvious when a number of lines consist entirely of clichés:

> Abandonnez au sol cette urne, humble trophée
> Qu'un agreste concours valut à l'art D'Orphée
>
> J'irai porter des fleurs aux sombres eaux du Styx
> Mais toi, roi de l'Oubli, ô fleuve du Léthé...

Other lines further suggest that the theme of the poem should not be taken seriously.

> O nature étrangère et qui nous vient d'ailleurs

is a tautology whose terms: "étrangère," "d'ailleurs," vaguely echo themes of alienation. In a context of parody, however, the use of a tautology does not serve a poetic function (such as, for example, emphasis of a lyrical theme). Rather, it underlines the empty character of the tautological clichés. Other lines contain predictable antitheses:

> Je meurs de te connaître et meurs de t'ignorer.

The resulting comical effect of *déjà vu* is even more pronounced in other sections of the poem. A convention of the neo-classical poetry is the formulation of philosophical questions concerning the enigma of being. This convention is represented here by three lines in which the city dweller addresses nature:

> O nature étrangère et qui nous vient d'ailleurs!
> ... ...
> D'où viens-tu, l'herbe? Qui donc es-tu l'espace?
> Je meurs en étranger, ô terre jamais lasse!

The first line is the previously cited tautology. The two questions in the second are patently inadequate as representatives of great philosophical problems. The first substitutes the word "l'herbe" for the expected *l'homme* (after "D'où viens-tu ..."), which transforms this traditional philosophical enigma into a frivolous question. The second, questioning the identity of space, is meaningless. The third line juxtaposes two grandiloquent phrases unrelated to each other, or to what precedes them. An accumulation of such structures, either clichés empty of meaning or pomposities, deflates its model by implying that it also exists uniquely on a verbal plane, empty of any lyrical or philosophical meaning.

One further remark may be made concerning this poem. It ends with two lines which are syntactically meaningless:

> Meurs! Daphné, du secret d'Apollon Confidente.
> Tremble aussitôt qu'on dort de l'approche des plantes. *[sic]*

The punctuation and wording of the 1921 edition of LC are identical with those of the 1960 edition. The two elements which are responsible for the lack of meaning of the lines are the period after "confidente," and the use of "dort" in the last line, for which no meaning of the verb *dormir* can possibly account. There are two possible explanations for this nonsensical syntax. One is that these two lines are given as the final absurdity of this poem, as if Jacob, carried along from line to line, and from cliché to cliché, had lost consciousness of meaning, and capped his parody with complete gibberish. The syntax, however, is so strange that typographical errors cannot be entirely ruled out: it is possible that the 1960 edition perpetuated an error in the original text.

The interpretation of elements which recall a model is a delicate matter: a resemblance, structural or thematic, to a literary model is not proof of intent to parody. The principle involved is that of the primacy of the context. Satirical parodies are satirical, not because they allude to literary models, but rather because these models are deflated in the immediate context through the use of humorous devices. Suzanne Bernard remarks that "Une de mes journées" (CD, p. 176) imitates "assez drôlement l'inspiration et la forme de 'A Une Heure du matin,' [one of Baudelaire's prose poems] and adds: "on peut voir dans ce ... poème une imitation assez perverse de la banalité." [7] Banal elements in poetic contexts are synonymous with humor for a great many critics. This as well as the structural resemblance to the Baudelaire poem, lead Miss Bernard to conclude that Jacob's poem is a parody. A comparison of the two texts, however, suggests that the humor of Jacob's poem does not derive from the presence of banal elements *per se* but rather from the treatment of these elements in the poem and that, furthermore, this humor is not incompatible with lyricism, so that both texts, that of Baudelaire and that of Jacob, are lyrical.

Jacob's text is far briefer than that of Baudelaire and is written as one paragraph:

> Avoir voulu puiser de l'eau à la pompe avec deux pots bleus, avoir été pris de vertige à cause de la hauteur de l'échelle; être revenu parce que j'avais un pot de trop et n'être pas retourné à la pompe à cause du vertige; être sorti pour acheter un plateau pour ma lampe parce qu'elle laisse le pétrole l'abandonner; n'avoir pas trouvé d'autres plateaux que des plateaux à thé, carrés, peu convenables pour des lampes et être sorti sans plateau. M'être dirigé vers la bibliothèque publique et m'être

---

[7] Suzanne Bernard, *op. cit.*, p. 629.

> aperçu en chemin que j'avais deux faux cols et pas de cravate; être rentré à la maison; être allé chez M. Vildrac pour lui demander une Revue et n'avoir pas pris cette Revue parce que M. Jules Romains y dit du mal de moi. N'avoir pas dormi à cause d'un remords, à cause des remords et du désespoir.

The following is the half of the third paragraph of Baudelaire's poem that Jacob's text particularly resembles, which also consists of a series of phrases alternating *avoir* and *être,* and the concluding paragraph of the poem:

> Horrible vie! Horrible vie! Récapitulons la journée: avoir vu plusieurs hommes de lettres, dont l'un m'a demandé si l'on pouvait aller en Russie par voie de terre (il prenait sans doute la Russie pour une île); avoir disputé généreusement contre le directeur d'une revue, qui à chaque objection répondait: "—C'est ici le parti des honnêtes gens," ce qui implique que tous les autres journaux sont rédigés par des conquins; avoir salué une vingtaine de personnes, dont quinze me sont inconnues; avoir distribué des poignées de main dans la même proportion, et cela sans avoir pris la précaution d'acheter des gants; être monté pour tuer le temps, pendant une averse, chez une sauteuse qui m'a prié de lui dessiner un costume de *Vénustre...*
>
> Mécontent de tous et mécontent de moi, je voudrais bien me racheter et m'énorgueillir un peu dans le silence et la solitude de la nuit. Âmes de ceux que j'ai aimés, âmes de ceux que j'ai chantés, fortifiez-moi, soutenez-moi, éloignez de moi le mensonge et les vapeurs corruptrices du monde; et veus, Seigneur mon Dieu! accordez-moi la grâce de produire quelques beaux vers qui me prouvent à moi-même que je ne suis pas le dernier des hommes, que je ne suis pas inférieur à ceux que je méprise. [8]

These two poems are similar, both structurally and thematically. Each is filled with details that express the pettiness, the meaningless trivialities that make up the day. The irritations (due

---

[8] Charles Baudelaire, *Œuvres* (Bibliothèque de la "Pléiade," 1954), p. 292.

to circumstances, to things, to bodily failings) evoked by Jacob are those which Baudelaire, in other poems than the one cited, called "le guignon;" those depicted by Baudelaire in this poem are petty annoyances, blows inflicted on his ego by men he considers his inferiors. Each poem is lyrical because it expresses the torment of its author. Each treats these themes somewhat differently. What seems particularly anti-poetic (or prosaic) about Jacob's poem is that such words as *pompe, échelle, pots bleus, plateaux à thé,* whose connotations are particularly utilitarian, are used in a context which might seem more suitable to slapstick comedy than to lyricism: the events narrated by Jacob consist of a series of petty failures, whose causes verge on the ludicrous. The ladder at the well is too high; the petrol leaves its lamp; the narrator is unable to purchase a very common article; he puts on two false collars and no ties, etc. The mechanical aspects of this repetition of failure, as Bergson pointed out in *Le Rire,* are the very essence of comedy. The narrator of Jacob's poem becomes a pitiable, ludicrous figure, and the smile or laughter of the reader prevents him momentarily from identifying himself with the narrator. The irony of the central passage in Baudelaire's poem, on the other hand, is directed against others, whom the narrator depicts as inferior to himself: therefore, the reader can share his anguish.

Yet paradoxically, despite its comical aspects, the sorrow evoked by Jacob's narrator is, if anything, deeper and more hopeless than that evoked by Baudelaire. This is clearly brought out by the different conclusions, which also illustrate the differences in style and theme between the two poems. Baudelaire's ends with a hope of redemption: even the trivialities and annoyances of the day shall not have been in vain if they can serve as the material for a beautiful poem, whose composition will prove his own worth to its author. These sentiments are expressed in a rhetorical invocation, written in a majestically structured *période* whose rhythm underscores the hope of redemption expressed by the narrator. Jacob's poem ends with a triple enumeration, "à cause d'un remords, à cause des remords et du désespoir," which sums up both the anguish of the poem, its hopelessness, and the density of its style, giving each word maximum expressiveness. The terms "remords" and "desespoir" constitute the only lyrical note in the poem. Their location at its closure, the repetition of "remords," sum up its mood and underline the theme. Both the rhetorical rhythm of the *période* and the sentiments it expresses, raise the level of style of the Baudelaire poem by identifying it with the tradition of lyrical poetry written in the noble style. In Jacob's poem, on the other hand, the anguish arising from the banal and the prosaic is unrelieved and for that reason, expressed through banal and prosaic occurrences and a dense, direct style. The total effect is similar to the power of litote. The comical narrator, dwelling in a hostile world he cannot cope with, antedates Charlie Chaplin's tramp, but the comedy is very similar. If Jacob's poem reminds the reader of Baudelaire's, it should be seen — not as a parody of it — but rather as a way of bringing Baudelaire's theme up to date, of translating the anguish of modern man, ludicrous and pitiable, who at night, can find no hope which will sustain him to face another day, not even hope in art.

Creative Parodies

When elements which both evoke and deflate a model dominate a poem, both statistically and esthetically, the poem is a satirical parody. However, clichés which recall a model can appear only in sections of the poem or may not represent the most significant esthetic device in the poem. Such clichés fulfill a variety of functions other than that of deflating a model. These functions, which characterize creative parodies, are responsible for the variety of possible interpretations to which these poems are subject.

The interpretation of creative parodies must be based entirely on elements internal to the poem. One indication that a text is a creative parody is the presence of incongruities. For example, one text in LC, p. 70 — "A M. Modigliani pour lui prouver que je suis un poète" — is composed of two sections, which clash stylistically and thematically. The first consists of a lengthy preamble, of the type often found in romantic poetry, depicting a symbolic décor (here, an evocation of clouds). It is a parody aiming its shafts at a number of poetic styles, accumulating pell mell clichés of poetic diction such as the periphrases "les charmes de mes songes"; precious metaphors such as the following personification of a cloud which, chased by the wind, releases thunder and lightning :"Il se tourne, rugit et lance un pied d'airain"; or solemn overwritten metaphors such as:

> Le noir sommet des monts s'endort sur les terrasses
> Sillons creusés par Dieu pour cacher les humains

which are meant to suggest meaningless statements masquerading as profound metaphors (the first image suggests nothing except a black mountain top falling asleep over the surrounding terrain; and the definition of the valleys proposed by the second line, unrelated to anything else in the preamble, remains totally inexplicable). As in the satirical parodies considered in the previous section, it is the accumulation of this sort of image that renders the poem parodic. The second section of the poem, however, changes tone entirely:

> Au lieu de femme un jour j'avais rencontré Dieu
> Compagnon qui brode mon être
> Sans que je puisse le connaître.
> Il est le calme et la gaîté
> Il donne la sécurité
> Et pour célébrer ses mystères
> Il m'a nommé son secrétaire
> Or pendant les nuits je déchiffre
> Un papier qu'il chargea de chiffres
> Que de sa main même il écrit
> Et déposa dans mon esprit
> Dans l'aquarium des airs vivent les démons indiscrets
> Qui font écrouler le nuage pour lui voler notre secret.

Some of the allusions in this section are autobiographical: the first line refers to Jacob's conversion; the "chiffres" which the "lyrical I" in the poem is deciphering refer to Jacob's project, never abandoned, of interpreting the symbolism of the Bible in terms of the Kabbalah. The lyrical qualities of the passage, however, stem from its style rather than from the autobiographical nature of the allusions. The most significant contrast between the two sections results from the simplicity of expression and the directness of the second section. Except for the final two lines, its vocabulary is that of everyday speech and is entirely devoid of poetic diction. The syntax and grammar are equally simple. The final two lines result in still another contrast: one moves from an evocation of peace and serenity to one of malevolence. The allusion to "démons indiscrets" (the adjective is completely unexpected), together with the metaphor "dans l'aquarium des airs," and the final line turn the atmosphere into an ocean thickly populated with demons whose characteristic evil function is not the temptation of men into evil, but rather that of being ever present spies from whom it is impossible to keep any secrets. The image of the *nuage,* which in the first section of the poem was a pretext for clichés, participates in the transformation: the cloud becomes the dwelling place of innumerable demons, a symbol of their ubiquitous presence. The technique of the entire second section is one of understatement, suggesting more than is made explicit, giving each word maximum expressiveness, and resulting in a very powerful, because restrained, kind of lyricism. The poem juxtaposes two entirely different styles: the lyrical style of the second section, and the parodic style of the first. The clichés of the first section are made to appear even more inflated and devoid of meaning when their parodic quality is underlined by the simplicity of style in the second section.

In some creative parodies, the link with a literary model is very slight, perhaps limited to an allusion. A title such as "Roman feuilleton" (CD, p. 89) or "Encore le roman feuilleton" (CD, p. 118) leads to anticipation of parody of these genres. A proper name such as Fantômas, the main protagonist of the Allain and Souvestre series, evokes its atmosphere of melodrama. A formula such as "Il y avait une fois..." ("Conte de Noël" CD, I, p. 76), the consecrated beginning of all fairy tales, brings them to mind. A character in a poem can reveal himself through his speech as the protagonist of a type of novel (very much in the same way as dialogue serves to place the social milieu of the psychology of a character in "realistic" novels). The following remarks, for example:

> "Vous ne me reconnaissez pas, dit-il en cette langue. Je suis le mari de votre bonne anglaise!"
> ("Roman d'aventures," CD, p. 128);

> —Monsieur, Diane est mon épouse et notre enfant est chez sa mère.
> ("Le Nom," CD, p. 156).

identify the protagonists since the suggestion of complicated melodramatic situations — names, types of plot — are all characteristic of popular novels. Another comment identifies the protagonist, an adolescent youth hesitating to enter, for the first time in his life, a house of ill repute, as the first person narrator of an autobiographical novel, a *Bildungsroman:*

> ...mon ami et moi nous errâmes longtemps autour de la maison et nous ne nous décidâmes à frapper de nouveau qu'après la nuit.
> ("La Vie d'étudiant," CD, p. 154).

Such allusions can serve as the point of departure for a poem which develops in a manner totally unrelated to the suggested model; for example, the poem entitled "Marcel Proust," in CD, II, p. 18:

> ... Anna de Noailles arriva sur la plage avec une petite capote de satin blanc à brides ornées de violettes comme on les portait cette année-là. Mendès et moi, nous avions deux vieilles cousines qui ne manquèrent pas d'apporter dans du papier des maquereaux séchés brisés comme des arcs-en-ciel. Elles étaient avares, etc.

The poem is quoted in full. The title suggests similarities with Proust's style. The three periods at the beginning imply that what follows is (or might have been) a fragment lifted from Proust. A number of elements in the poem can be interpreted as patterned after characteristics of Proust's style or themes. The name Anna de Noailles suggests Proust's interest in high society. (She is named, not because she is a poetess, but because she is of noble birth). The comparison between the "maquereaux" and the "arcs-en-ciel" recalls Proust's frequent metaphors and comparisons. The description of the hats is reminiscent of Proust's interest in fashion. The entire tone of the anecdote brings mind the type of conversation sometimes engaged in by some of Proust's characters — at the Verdurin house, for example, or at Balbec (given the allusion to "la plage"). The entire poem appears to be a parody of Proust's style, ridiculing it by reducing it to a collection of trivialities and petty gossip. On the other hand, it might be argued that nothing about the poem is particularly Proustian except for the allusion in the title and that indeed, there is only an effect of superposition, without any real link between the Proustian style and Jacob's poem. Particularly glaring is the absence of comical exaggeration, distortions or accumulations rendering a model ridiculous. Furthermore, many other poems ("Cet Allemand était fou d'art...") center around anecdotes to which no particular significance can be assigned. In this case, the three periods at the beginning of the poem, and the hiatus between the title and the rest of the poem, underline its fundamental ambiguity.

A poem can exploit allusions to a literary model for the sake of fantasy, for the pleasure of telling a complicated anecdote full of unexpected developments, as in "Sir Élizabeth (prononcez sœur)" in CD, p. 120:

> La cité de Happney est détruite, hélas! Il ne reste plus qu'un mur entre deux tours carrées, deux tours qui ont l'air de fermes ou de citernes. Ce furent des facultés d'enseignement: elles sont vides! il ne reste plus... il ne reste plus qu'une porte d'écurie et des crevasses, hélas! avec des pavés couverts de ronces. Le chef de gare est encore là pourtant, c'est lui qui m'a conté l'histoire de sir Élizabeth. Sir Élizabeth était du sexe féminin mais elle dut se faire homme de peine. Sir Élizabeth prit part à un concours de poésie. A cette époque, en Amérique, le sexe féminin n'avait pas l'idée d'être poète. Sir Élizabeth fut couronnée et eut droit au double buste de chaque côté d'une porte d'écurie. La porte existe encore; les deux bustes sont abîmés par le temps, hélas! Sir Élizabeth fut troublée par le sculpteur qui avait fait son buste et elle lui révéla son sexe, mais le sculpteur la repoussa, parce qu'elle avait trompé la cité. Alors, sir Élizabeth s'engagea dans la milice et se fit tuer.

The beginning of the poem simulates the structure associated with the opening of many nineteenth century novels, and this sets the stage for the story through a complex interplay for setting, narrator, flashbacks: a person returns to a place he had known long before; he discovers it has changed; he meets someone who tells him what has transpired since his departure, thus becoming the narrator of the tale. In the remainder of the poem, such exclamations as "hélas" or marginal comments, simulate the reaction of the traveler to the tale. In addition, the plot, a doomed love story which fails through a series of unlikely events, is also characteristic of many nineteenth century popular novels. In a novel, however, the development is leisurely, in order to portray the events as fully as possible; both the structure and plot are used to create suspense and to involve the reader emotionally. The main device in the poem, on the other hand, is the rapid juxtaposition of totally unexpected developments in plot or incongruous word combinations. The accelerated rhythm of the poem, which condenses a series of unlikely occurrences within a few lines, is similar in effect to the exploitation, in films of the early sixties, for comic effects, of the rhythm of early films, in which one scene succeeds another with great jerkiness and abruptness. No attempt is made to involve the reader emotionally. Instead, he is constantly surprised by the rapidity of the developments. Verbal inventions also contribute to this effect: the bilingual pun in the title, which is also an oxymoron; the further exploitation of the pun when Sir Élizabeth becomes "homme de peine": a double pun since Sir Élizabeth is a woman, and since the pun is developed literally in the rest of the poem; the entire "sexe féminin" considered as a single person. A number of elements are inserted primarily for comic effect; for example, the prize for the poet laureate consists of two busts on either side of a stable door, and the moral rigidity of the sculptor who refuses to wed "Sir Élizabeth" because she pretended to be a man in order to enter the contest. Such a poem surprises by its absurd, comic, and delightful inventions.

The reverse effect is also found: a very brief poem can condense or suggest the typical unfolding of the plot of a longer work. Two of the briefest are:

> Une princesse habitait dans un quart de poire.
> (Untitled, CD, p. 241);

> Adam et Ève sont nés à Quimper.
> (Untitled, CD, p. 240).

The first one would be a suitable beginning for a fairy tale, but here it is the entire fairy tale. The lack of development results in surprise and humor, as does the dwelling place selected.

The second poem can be interpreted variously. It can suggest a capsule summary of the eternal renewal of the story of the fall. As an aphorism, it is a reflection on the unchanging nature of man. As a comment on Quimper, it suggests that Quimper is a suitable locale for the fall, either because of its iniquity or because it is a garden of Eden. These possibilities are far from exhaustive or mutually exclusive. Again, as in "L'enfant, l'éfant...," the ultimate appeal is to the imagination. The extreme density of these two texts, contributing to their ambiguity, is the source of their poetic value.

Occasionally, as in "Encore le roman feuilleton" (CD, p. 12), the expectations built up by the allusion to a literary model are systematically frustrated by the remainder of the poem. The citation could begin anywhere since the entire poem is constructed along similar lines. The two final paragraphs are quoted here:

> Robert s'appelait plutôt Hippolyte. Il eût été habillé à la dernière mode, s'il y avait eu une dernière mode, mais il n'y a pas de dernière mode; alors, il était habillé comme tout le monde, c'est-à-dire mal. Robert eût été capable de faire huit cents kilomètres en auto pour aller dire à l'ami de ses amis: "J'ai le bonjour à vous souhaiter de la part de M. Tel," car Robert était bon, mais il n'avait pas d'ami.
>
> Robert s'installa à table et mangea comme il n'avait pas mangé depuis longtemps, c'est-à-dire qu'il mangea peu, car il mangeait toujours beaucoup. Ai-je dit qu'il mangea bien? Or, il mangeait le plus souvent médiocrement, mais cela lui était indifférent. Robert ne faisait rien pour ne pas perdre de temps à travailler: il le perdait peut-être autrement. S'il eût eu quelque tâche, il n'eût pas su s'en tirer, aussi n'en prenait-il pas. Robert ne faisait rien, ce qui vaut mieux que de faire mal, et ceci ne l'empêchait pas de mal faire. Mais laissons Robert à Chartres.

The title suggests a spoof, or an evocation, of a *roman feuilleton*. But the poem does not in any way attempt to develop a situation or anecdote — from the beginning to the end or from one sentence to the other. Instead, it is made up of a string of clichés of daily conversation. Its principle of organization is to empty every cliché enunciated of its anticipated meaning, either by following it with another expression opposite in meaning or negating the existence of the thing mentioned. To be dressed "comme tout le monde" connotes: "to be well dressed"; but in the poem, "être habillé comme tout le monde" means "to be badly dressed." To eat "comme il n'avait pas mangé depuis longtemps" usually means: "to eat well." Again, here, it means the opposite. The final paragraph refines on this technique by contradicting the contradictions, so that all meaning is lost. What is under attack then, is not the *roman feuilleton* but rather the clichés of daily conversation and, beyond that, the concept that words must correspond to a stable and predictable reality. Both words and reality are negated in the poem through a systematic kind of illogic that affirms their illusory existence. Humor and illogic (or nonsense) undermine some of the most fundamental assumptions abont words and reality.

Conventional parodies are, by definition, highly predictable: once the model is recognised, once the style of the parodist is set, the rest of the text is in the same vein. The earmark of Jacob's creative parodies, on the other hand, is that they are highly unpredictable. At their best, they achieve the density, the complexity, characteristic of the best poetic utterances. One of Jacob's most effective, and least classifiable parodies is "Fausses nouvelles! fosses nouvelles!" (CD, p. 25), in which a patently absurd event is related with deadpan seriousness:

> A une représentation de *Pour la couronne*, à l'Opéra, quand Desdémone chante "Mon père est à Goritz et mon cœur à Paris," on a entendu un coup de feu dans une loge de cinquième galerie, puis un second aux fauteuils et instantanément des échelles de cordes se sont déroulées; un homme a voulu descendre des combles: une balle l'a arrêté à la hauteur du balcon. Tous les spectateurs étaient armés et il s'est trouvé que la salle n'était pleine que de... et de... Alors, il y a eu des assassinats du voisin, des jets de pétrole enflammé. Il y a eu des sièges de loges, le siège de la scène, le siège d'un strapontin et cette bataille a duré dix-huit jours. On a peut-être ravitaillé les deux camps, je ne sais, mais ce que je sais fort bien c'est que les journalistes sont venus pour un si horrible spectacle, que l'un d'eux étant souffrant, y a envoyé madame sa mère et que celle-ci a été beaucoup

intéressée par le sang-froid d'une (sic) jeune gentilhomme français qui a tenu dix-huit jours dans une avant-scène sans rien prendre qu'un peu de bouillon. Cet épisode de la guerre des Balcons a beaucoup fait pour les engagements volontaires en Province. Et je sais, au bord de ma rivière, sous mes arbres, trois frères en uniformes tout neufs qui se sont embrassés les yeux secs, tandis que leurs familles cherchaient des tricots dans les armoires des mansardes.

The title is mimetic of a newsboy, hawking a special edition. This poem contains elements that make it analogous to almost every type of parody considered in this chapter, Interpreted as a satirical parody, it has a number of posible targets. One is newspaper style, suggested by the title or by its deadpan style. Language itself is another possible target since, in a number of places, the poem simultaneously relates an event on one level while dissolving it into nonsense on another. This is true, for example, of the series of puns contained in "Il y a eu des sièges de loges, le siège de la scène, le siège d'un strapontin et cette bataille a duré dix-huit jours," in which "siège" means either "seat" (as in a theater) or "siege" (as in an attack). Either meaning fits, or both, so that each fragment can be read in a number of ways: "there were seats in the loges" or "the loges were besieged"; "there was the siege of a folding seat" or "there was the seat of a folding seat"; etc. The evident disproportion between the possible meanings of "siège," the ridicule of a siege either of a loge or of a folding seat, as well as the final disproportion between the objects of attack and the duration of the battle, function as a metalinguistic commentary, reducing the entire edifice to absurdity. Furthermore, in "... la salle n'était pleine que de... et de..." there is a lack of communication which might be interpreted to mean that the suppressed details are evident, unspeakable, or unnecessary. Literary evocations of bravery during wartime represent still another target. The last lines of the poem may contain an allusion to the scene in Corneille's play *Horace* when the Horace and Curiace brothers go off, dry-eyed and resolute, to war. The allusion to the war of "balconies" suggests similarly labelled historical episodes: "the war of the Balkans" in 1912 and 1913, or "the war of Roses" in England. On another level, the poem can be taken as a satire commenting on the futility of war reducing its motivating force to absurd proportions. The poem can also seem merely an imaginative, somewhat humorous anecdote, an example of sick humor, perhaps, or fantasy for its own sake. Ultimately, however, all these comments fall short of the poem. Its wealth of details and precise location testify to a kind of realism that is destined to make the unreal seem plausible. Each reader supplies his own interpretation; yet the poem resists all: it exists, its central ambiguities the source of its appeal.

Chapter III

IMAGERY

The term image designates a word or expression which evokes a representation in the mind of the reader. The characteristic function of an image is to make the reader see, to evoke the sensuous characteristics of an object or scene, that is, to concretise. The broadest distinctions between images are those between literal images and figurative ones. A literal image represents itself only whereas a figurative image either compares an object or quality with another object or quality (simile) or substitutes a concrete expression for an abstract concept (metaphor). Literal imagery in Jacob's poetry can further be broken down into two additional categories. The first consists of images, generally suggested through concrete nouns, which evoke real objects or scenes, but cause them to acquire connotations beyond the visual or sensuous representations evokes. These I have called called "substantives effective in a number of way at once." The second category consists of images which display the disfigurement of reality associated with dreams or are totally invented, but which, like other literal images, represent only themselves. These I have called called "oneiric" or "visionary" images. The term "affective" indicates that an image appeals primarily to the emotions, and "expressive" indicates that it is particularly apt in translating the meaning at hand.

Literal Imagery — Substantives effective in a number of ways at once.

Monique Parent has pointed out the particular importance of substantives in prose poetry, where, along with devices such as a concentric structure, which she identifies as characteristic of the prose poem, "poetic diction" compensates for the relative lack of meter in prose poetry (compared to lyric or verse poetry). Her conclusions are based on a study of the poems of Paul Fort, Francis Jammes, the André Gide of *Les Nourritures terrestres,* and Saint John Perse, all of which are characterized by an evident effort to set poetic usage apart from spoken usage, both in syntax and vocabulary.[1] Such distinctions between levels of style are totally alien to Jacob's poetry, where elegant, inelegant, "poetic," or "anti-poetic" language can all be found in the same poem. Moreover, Jacob does not necessarily compensate for a lack of meter through the use of concentric structures or the like. Nevertheless, substantives are given great prominence in his poetry. Their value as images (in his texts) derives from stylistic devices, or from associations made implicit or explicit in the poem that charge them with many kinds of suggestions and force them to mean more than they do ordinarily. The literal meaning of the substantive remains unchanged, but the additional connotations permit the poet to reformulate lyrical or archetypal themes.

How effective this use of substantives can be may be shown by the analysis of a prose passage from Jacob's collection of essays and short stories entitled *Le Roi de Béotie,* p. 228-9. "Béotien" is used to designate an uncultured person indifferent to artistic beauty. The title thus refers to Jacob's efforts away from traditional "artistic" beauty, towards an expressive "prosaism." A number of the allusions in the text are autobiographical: Jacob had been hit by a car in 1919, and had subsequently contracted pneumonia during his stay in Lariboisière, a famous hospital in Paris:

> Hôpital, mausolée des vivants, tu es entre deux gares, gare toi-même pour les départs d'où on ne revient pas. Je m'agenouille en pensée devant ton seuil; je remercie Dieu qui m'a laissé parmi les hommes de la terre. Sur ce banc, pour moi, la faiblesse et la fatigue ressemblent à l'agonie. Tête si faible encore, et ça commande à tout, la tête! pauvres membres comme vieillis à pauvre tête si

---

[1] See *St. John Perse et quelques devanciers* (Paris, 1960), p. 24.

faible toujours, si faible encore. Agonie! la fatigue! oh! la faiblesse. Ohé! les gens pressés des autos, vous mourrez! vous mourrez! ohé! les jeunes et les vieux, vous mourrez! les femmes popotes et celles de la grande vie, les bas-bleus, vous mourrez mes amis! les gens des autos, écoutez! écoutez donc mon glas, je dis que vous mourrez. Je viens de l'apprendre à l'hôpital et je vous le crie boulevard Magenta. Vous mourrez, nous mourrons, O mot effroyablement vrai, ô mot de vérité, de seule vérité, mot qu'on ne peut remuer et qu'il faut toucher avec le doigt de la pensée, vous mourrez. Mais écoutez-moi donc au lieu de filer: nous allons mourir tout à l'heure.

The passage is a monologue consisting mainly of a succession of apostrophes and exclamations in which substantives predominate, punctuated by the repetition of "nous mourrons, vous mourrez." The scene, suggested sketchily but concretely, is immediately recognized and visualized by anyone who has been in a city: a man, here sitting on a bench, is urgently addressing passers by, all going about their business, self-absorbed, hurrying ("filer" is a slang term for walking in a hurry), indifferent to the message of the speaker. A number of phrases in the text make it clear that he has had a close brush with death: "Je remercie Dieu qui m'a laissé parmi les hommes de la terre"; "sur ce banc, pour moi, la faiblesse et la fatigue ressemblent à l'agonie." It is his newly discovered sense of his own mortality, and the accompanying fear and anguish, that he is seeking to convey to the passers-by. The scene is clearly situated at the level of the ordinary, the daily event. The setting is a precise one in Paris, alluding to a well-known street, "boulevard Magenta." Except for "seuil," "glas," and "agonie," which are examples of poetic diction, the vocabulary is derived entirely from spoken usage, even including a number of expressions which are colloquial or slang: "filer," already mentioned, as well as "popotes," in the expression "les femmes popotes" (*popote*, a familiar term for soup, designates a hausfrau type of woman, as opposed to one of "la grande vie"). Much of the syntax is modelled on conversational turns: "nous allons mourir tout à l'heure" (we are going to die very soon); "et ça commande à tout la tête" (and it governs everything, the head); "je viens de l'apprendre à l'hôpital" (I have just learned it in the hospital); "mais écoutez-moi donc au lieu de filer" (but listen to me instead of hurrying by." These factors, however, make it particularly easy for the reader to project himself into the text, to imagine that he is being addressed directly by the person on the bench.

Other elements in the passage reinforce its affective qualities. the primary one is the use of apostrophes and exclamations. These translate the writer's emotion and his sense of urgency, and they also make it clear that he is addressing each passer-by and hence each reader on an immediate and personal level. The repetitions of "nous mourrons, vous mourrez" and of "agonie" underline the theme of death, and confer upon it an obsessional quality. "Glas" meaning death knell and "agonie" (the final agony) are particularly strong affective terms. The periphrasis "pour les départs d'où on ne revient pas" (for the departures from which there is no return) underlines the finality of the last voyage. The next to the last sentence, a classical *période* "O mot effroyablement vrai, ô mot de vérité...") recalls both the rhythm and the theme of Bossuet's sermons on death, and brings literary reminiscences to bear on the text. Finally, the last sentence: "Mais écoutez-moi donc au lieu de filer: nous allons mourir tout à l'heure" (but listen to me instead of hurrying by: we are all going to die very soon) sums up the emotions of the passage: the indifference of the passers-by, and the despair of the speaker. Moreover the "nous" in that phrase referring to the reader, the passers-by and the speaker, together with "tout à l'heure," summarizes both the immediacy of death and its universality.

The urban nature of the setting, as well as the terms in the first sentence in which a hospital is successively compared with a mausoleum for the living, a way station between two stations, and a railroad station, deserve further comment. The poetry of the early part of the century is filled with similar evocations of the city or of the technology associated with industrialisation. These evocations correspond to a need which the poets felt, even if not articulated, to find a symbolism, suited to the predominantly industrial character of the age, that would replace the diction of archetypal themes based on an agrarian society. The railroad stations constitute a particularly appropriate vehicle for the theme of death, which archetypally is a final journey. Other aspects of this theme are brought to mind by the series of metaphors of the first sentence: the brevity of one's stay in a station; its function as a point of arrival and departure, of transition; the anxiety which accompanies any journey, etc. All these can be articulated in symbolic terms, but these associations are so intimately part of the experience of railroads and journeys that they can be transferred from the word to the archetypal themes almost without thought. These associations are inevitable in this text filled with so many evocations of the theme of death, but the passage brings to mind other aspects of urban life as well. Most importantly, the failure of the man on the bench to attract the attention of the passers-by, and their indifference, suggests the essential loneliness (we might even call it alienation) of modern urban life.

The deliberately "familiar" aspects of this text mask its highly elaborate character. It succeeds, however, in charging a familiar scene and objects with symbolic, archetypal, and affective connotations. Similar results can be achieved with far greater economy, through a variety of structural patterns of syntax which call attention to the poetic value of the substantives. Through elliptical patterns, for example, each object named can be made to carry the value of an image; as when a line of poetry is composed of substantives only, with no grammatical connectives:

>   Pour un bout de temps
>   Printemps.
>
>   Pivoine, glycine!
>   ("Avril infernal," DP, p. 27).

The two details: "pivoine, glycine": are chosen for their general associations. Simply naming these substantives evokes a field of associated commonplaces: fragility, beauty. The immediate context confers additional connotations. Spring suggests that the flowers are the traditional symbols of hope and joy, of rebirth. The title, however, is an oxymoron, since spring is normally associated with joy, rather than with anything infernal. Therefore the title confers upon the flowers and their usual associations a quality of foreboding, of threat.

A similar pattern is an exclamation containing a substantive and its modifiers:

Ah! les grands poissons blancs sur la nappe de verre
("Plainte du mauvais garçon," LC, p. 62).

This image is one of a series in which the "mauvais garçon" of the title evokes the home which he regrets. Out of context, the incongruous juxtaposition of "poissons blancs" and "nappe de verre" lends the image a surrealistic quality which it would not ordinarily possess. Various interpretations come to mind: the "poissons blancs" might be cooked fish, or serving dishes in the form of fish, or doilies, at the dinner table. Through contiguity, the image evokes a home, dinnertime, a whole ambiance of bourgeois cosiness and comfort. The "verre" in "nappe de verre" may also be explained by a desire to pun on *vert,* meaning green. This is all the more likely since the line before those quoted ends with "roses." The term designates the flowers, but does not exclude the possibility of the evocation of a pretty combination of colors, composed with the eye of a painter.

In a similar manner, an elliptical phrase composed of substantives can be included in a sentence:

Que l'on m'enterre entre pierre et goëmon...
("La Mort, IV," HdC, p. 164).

"Goëmon" is a Breton term, designating a kind of alga. The two substantives, "pierre et goëmon" evoke Brittany, its language and landscape, in a context expressing nostalgia for the place of one's birth. The lyrical theme of "regrets" is suggested with great economy in both this example and the preceding one.

An entire poem can be composed around such metonymic evocations, as for example, "Le Départ," in LC, p. 56:

Adieu l'étang et toutes mes colombes
Dans leur tour et qui mirent gentiment
Leur soyeux plumage au col blanc qui bombe
    Adieu l'étang.

Adieu maison et ses toitures bleues
Où tant d'amis, dans toutes les saisons
Pour nous revoir avaient fait quelques lieues,
    Adieu maison.

Adieu le linge à la haie en piquants
Près du clocher! oh! que de fois le peins-je
Que tu connais comme t'appartenant
Adieu le linge!

The remainder of the poem is composed according to the same pattern. Each detail serves to build up a carefully stylized and somewhat idealized image of the poet's home village. The details are chosen both for their general associations (associated commonplaces), and for the highly personalized picture that they build: the pond, doves, home, church spire, all conventional symbols of home, peace, tranquillity. The other details provide an even more personal note: the "spire" which the poet painted, etc.

Opposite in technique, though similar in result, is the enumeration or accumulation of substantives. This is found in both prose and verse poetry. An example is the poem entitled "Purgatoire," in HdC, p. 70:

Tous les à vif de ta vie
les journées de dure mélancolie
la faim, la fatigue avec les clous dans les souliers
la marche en sueur, sans boire
le froid au vestibule de l'impossible gloire
la maladie de l'estomac dans des chambres noires
trois sous pour le métro et dix pour un timbre
là-dessus les impôts et sans que tu regimbes
le souffle court à l'hôpital
l'injure et les moqueurs, tout ce que l'on ravale
les trahisons d'amis, les triomphes rieurs
l'horrible pitié des meilleurs
ma vie d'accidents et tous mes bons vouloirs
le pauvre pitre sur fond noir
les accessits, les accessoires
tout ça n'est rien auprès du Purgatoire.

The effort of Jacob to situate poetic utterances in the everyday, the commonplace, is clearly evident in this poem. Many of the details selected, such as "la faim," "la fatigue avec les clous dans les souliers," "la marche en sueur," "trois sous pour le métro et dix pour un timbre" present some unpleasant aspects of the penury of a struggling artist. Taken singly, the directness and concreteness of each detail gives it great force. At the same time, the profusion of details gives the reader the impression that a complete portrait is being built up. The theme and technique are similar to those of "Une de mes journées": through the accumulation of details, and the parallel construction, the poem assumes the character of a monotonous litany of the pettiness and triviality of daily life, which is a source of deep despair. This lyrical theme is expressed personally, since the details chosen reflect a uniquely personal experience. For example, melancholy, in French literature, is generally associated with a kind of voluptuous sadness; here, it is preceded by the adjective "dure." Pity is generally considered a worthy quality; in this text, it is treated as "horrible." Both of these translate the experience of an artist who has had to endure the snubs and contempt of others around him, as do other details such as "l'injure et les moqueurs," "les trahisons d'amis." The image of "le pauvre pitre sur fond noir" suggests the constant play acting of the poet, the constant clowning against a backdrop of sorrow. An additional effect is the contrast between the lengthy enumeration and the final litote: "tout ça n'est rien auprès du Purgatoire," which becomes hyperbolic, by expressing an additional theme: that earthly tribulations, painful as they are, cannot give an adequate idea of the torment one endures in Purgatory. The sound play of "les accessits, les accessoires" introduces a note of humor to this litany of despair, providing comic relief.

Jacob's literal images are generally concrete, and characteristically endowed with strong visual qualities. Both Belaval and Collier have mentioned that Jacob often composed poems with the eye of a painter, including in the text directions such as "en haut" or "en bas."[2] Many poems, entitled "Tableau" or "Peinture," or a variation of the term are primarily verbal equivalents of paintings, as is the following, called "Peinture," from CD, II, p. 187:

> C'est sur le Pont Neuf que se tient la foire. Fard des femmes, tomates, radis, pivoines, tout est en rouge, sauf des œufs, des fromages. Sur des trapèzes volent les acrobates qui cachent un instant le soleil.

---

[2] Yvon Belaval, *La Rencontre avec Max Jacob* (Paris, 1946), p. 100; S. J. Collier, "Max Jacob's *Le Cornet à dés*," *French Studies*, XI (April 1957), 152.

The Pont Neuf is one of the oldest bridges in Paris, built between 1578 and 1607. Originally, it was lined with shops and frequented by *bateleurs* — traveling comedians. It was for a long time one of the favorite promenades of Parisians and, because, of its colorfulness, a favorite subject of painters and engravers. Locating the *Foire* on the Pont Neuf, recalling its earlier days, gives the poem a period atmosphere. As its title indicates, the poem is primarily an attempt to simulate in words the visual qualities of a painting, with its emphasis on colors, shapes, and the effect of arrested motion. Reds predominate, contrasting with the whites. In addition, the reds named, those of the women's make-up, tomatoes, radishes, peonies, differ from each other, as do the whites of the cheeses and eggs. The final image suggests both the suspended motion of the acrobats, caught in a moment of their flight, and their position in a two dimensional plane, that of the canvas hiding the sun.

Other poems, while retaining strong visual qualities, are more complex. Consider, for example, "Symbole artistique," in CD, II, p. 39:

> Entre deux montagnes japonaises, un fil est tendu — à peine si on voit le fil — c'est là que doit paraître et marcher le globe-trotter, d'ici il n'est pas plus gros qu'une abeille sur le ciel. Il va sur le fil précédé d'une brouette. Dans cette brouette est, dit-on, sa femme, les yeux bandés par peur du vertige, et ligotée emmaillotée pour qu'elle ne bouge pas. En dessous, c'est un abîme.

The visual images depicted are extremely precise, suggesting, given the adjective "japonaises" in the first line, the clarity and delicacy of line of a japanese print. Primarily, however, the nature, order, and precision of the details given, as well as the vocabulary, especially "vertige" and the final "abîme," (particularly important since it is the last word of the poem), create an effect of mounting suspense which, like the cliff hangers of the early part of the century, leaves the audience in mid-air, until the next episode. The suspense is left deliberately unresolved, and unresolvable, since the poem ends without conclusion. This can lead to a humorous interpretation of the text, as a mock thriller. The title suggests a number of additional interpretations. The image of the acrobat might be intended literally as a symbol of the precariousness of human existence or art. The precision of the details, however, tends to militate against such a literal interpretation. More plausibly, the significance of the title is to be found in the effect of unresolved suspense, the poem being an "artistic symbol" precisely because of its lack of resolution, and hence, its ambiguity.

In many poems, especially prose poems where lyrical themes are often translated by "objective" symbols, Jacob's personal interpretation of reality endows concrete visual images with special significance. Jacob pursued a lifelong interest in the occult, and especially, in the Kabbalah.[8] In his poems, Jacob's vision of the universe is reflected in images in which mundane realities are given as signs of spiritual ones. In all instances, the interpretation is given in the text: no reference to an external context is necessary. An explicit comment in the text, or a structural device, alerts the reader. A spectrum of possibilities exists.

In some poems, explicit references in the text illuminate the significance Jacob attributes to particular objects. These, for example, can link an object with a spiritual counterpart:

> Sur un ongle de pied: un cor! vous le taillez chaque matin: savez-vous que ses racines viennent de l'infini? Si je vous montrais... si je vous montrais cette chaîne de marbre blanc et de corail!...
> ("Science lunarienne, CD, II, p. 15);

> Il arrive quand tu ronfles que le monde matériel éveille l'autre.
> (Untitled, CD, p. 53);

> Un beau jour, il y eut comme la rayure d'ongle du tonnerre dans un nuage: les caissiers se trompèrent aux additions...
> ("Guerres et Amériques," DP, p. 196).

In each poem, an event in the real world corresponds to one in another world: a corn has roots in the infinite; one's snore may

---

[8] The fullest discussion of Jacob's interpretation of the Kabbalah is to be found in the introduction written by Blanchet to *La Défense de Tartufe* (Paris, 1964), pp. 16-20. See also René Plantier, *Max Jacob* (Desclée de Brouwer, 1972).

wake up beings in another world; cashiers' errors are linked to an event that also manifests itself in a thunderbolt. These relationships are metonymic, that is, the physical and spiritual events correspond to one another, as parts of one system. By evoking one, automatically, the poet also evokes, through contiguity, its physical or spiritual counterpart and hence the entire system to which it belongs. The contrast between the mundane, anti-poetic qualities of the objects named and their spiritual extensions constitutes the chief device of these poems. The resultant humor is compatible with the system of *correspondances* which they establish.

In other poems the link to the hidden, the mysterious world is less explicit. The reader must infer it. The following poem, called "Arrivée du démon," from CD, II, p. 164, is an example:

> Il y a un trou sous la table de toilette en pitchpin, dans le coin à droite, près de la fenêtre: c'est par là que montent les rats. Il y a une venelle obscure dans la rue de Vaugirard: c'est par là que sortirent les deux criminels qui me suivirent. Il y a un trou noir dans le ciel à l'endroit où le ciel rencontre l'horizon à gauche: c'est par là que sortent les nuages noirs qui l'envahissent.

The text presents a series of images of apertures (a hole under a table, a small street opening on rue Vaugirard, a black break in the sky) through which a number of unpleasant objects emerges: rats from the hole under the table, criminals from the "venelle," and black clouds from the break in the sky. The title suggests that each of the emerging objects is a concrete manifestation of evil. This impression is further reinforced by the nature of the objects themselves (criminals suggesting evil, rats reminiscent of the plague), as well as by the use of adjectives such as "obscur" or "noir" (repeated twice), which create an atmosphere of gloom and fear and also suggest an elementary symbolism (death). The weakness of the verbs ("il y a") gives prominence to the substantives, the images which are the focus of the poem. This feature is underlined by two other syntactical devices: the triple anaphora ("il y a, il y a, etc."); and the construction of each of the clauses beginning with "il y a," so that each segment adds a new thought to a sentence which would be complete without it, and hence adding a new, unexpected detail.[4] In each instance, the additional details supplied modify the substantive to which the text gives prominence, thereby concentrating attention on it. As elsewhere, the profusion and precision of details serves ends that are far from realism by forcing the reader to consider reality as possessing unsuspected depth and dimensions, here, as elsewhere, predominantly sinister.

The extent to which Jacob's system of *correspondances* is idiosyncratic can be inferred from the following two examples:

> Bas blancs rayés en travers (signe de démonialité) sur le tapis rouge...
> ("Péché dans la recherche de la vertu," DT, p. 116);

> A ceci vous reconnaîtrez une prostituée délivrée de la prison: trois fils noirs pendent sur son front, du bas de ses cheveux, vers ses sourcils.
> (Untitled, DP, p. 121).

The significance Jacob ascribes to the objects depicted is given in the text. Yet it remains a source of surprise, partly because of the arbitrariness of these implications and partly because such a system of interpretation is so alien to most readers, involving, in the first poem cited, a private demonology, and in the second, an equally private and impenetrable sign system. In this, as in the preceding examples, the objects or scenes are evoked through particularly colorful and precise visual images. Their concrete presence causes the significance Jacob ascribes to them to seem as much a part of reality as the objects which they depict. As a result, any ordinary object soon becomes suspect, because reality is never exactly what it seems and always hides an underlying dimension. What is of importance is not so much the cognitive content of Jacob's private metaphysical system, but rather, the dimensions it lends to objects, even the most commonplace ones.

---

[4] This type of sentence has been called by Riffaterre "phrase à rallonge." See *Le Style des Pléiades de Gobineau* (Columbia University Press, 1957), p. 110. Riffaterre notes that Ch. Bruneau calls this construction a "phrase à queue."

Again, the poem undermines assumptions about a stable world, in which appearance and reality are one.

Literal imagery: oneiric or visionary imagery.

Oneiric or visionary imagery is defined as literal — non figurative imagery that displays the distortion of reality associated with dream images: displacement of objects, deformed or mutilated objects, incongruous arrangements of objects, loss or change of identity, etc. [5] The two terms "oneiric" and "visionary" are not entirely synonymous, although Webster's definition of vision: "1. Something seen otherwise than by ordinary sight; something beheld as in a dream or ecstasy... 2. A visual image without corporeal presence..." points out that visionary images display tendencies toward hallucination or invention of objects which are similar to the disfigurement of reality associated with dream images. Although such images have always been present in literature and painting, twentieth century surrealism has given them particular prominence because of these images' spontaneity and complete unpredictability.

Any attempt to analyse or assign meaning to these images must take into account the high degree of invention involved, which results in the potential for surprise or obscurity. It has been stated that comic surprise and lyric surprise are potentially close: for this type of imagery, any distinction between the two is abolished. Many readers find a particular oneiric or visionary image merely grotesque, while others consider the same image beautiful. [6]

Oneric or visionary images are frequent in Jacob's work. They occur most often in his prose poetry, where they correspond to a tendency towards objectivity, the banishing of the "I" from the poem. They are lyrical, however, in that many express a world of nightmares and fears, of private or archetypal fantasies. Typical

---

[5] Such distortions have been catalogued in detail by Jacques Bousquet, *Les Thèmes du rêve dans la littérature romantique* (Paris, 1964), pp. 400-489.

[6] See for example the discussion of surrealist oneiric images in Jean Paulhan, *Jacob Cow le pirate ou si les mots sont des signes* (Paris, 1921), pp. 78-80.

of oneiric images with characteristic deformations or disfigurements are the following:

> Ce doigt qui me désigne, il lui manque une phalange.
> ("Désigné," VI, p. 77);

> ...mais sur les poteaux indicateurs, il y a les noms de toutes les communes de France écrits en toutes petites lettres.
> ("Misère," CD, II, p. 173);

> on étalait du noir au couteau sur la suie
> ("Nuit," FddL, n. p.).

The first image is an example of a mutilated object. The second, although humorous, displays a combination of oneiric themes: the incongruous juxtaposition of objects or change of function since the road markers, instead of pointing out the correct road, befuddle the traveler. The third is less explicitly oneiric. It might be interpreted as a joke, similar, for example, to the image of invisible negroes fighting in a dark tunnel. It occurs in a poem, however, entitled "Nuit," expressive of deep anguish, the spiritual night of the soul. All of the images which precede this one, as well as those which follow, translate this sentiment of complete hopelessness: "Plus rien plus rien en moi... Un grand banquet de néant..." In such a context, the image cited becomes, quite literally, an image of hell. The concretized blackness (since it is being spread, it has material qualities), the soot, and the knife suggest the décor of a private hell, although the soot might also suggest the ashes of hell. The theme of hell becomes explicit in the final image of the poem, a metaphor with visionary qualities: "Je suis un végétal ébranché vers l'enfer / dont les ailes jadis s'étendaient vers la mer" which evokes both the writer's present despair and his nostalgia for a lost state, perhaps of hope or innocence.

Alongside these images a great many others derive from medieval or conventional Christian representations of the supernatural. The use of this imagery, especially in poetry which is so innovative, constitutes a jarring anachronism. Moreover, the literal, corporal existence Jacob attributes to supernatural beings, such as demons or angels, implies a literal interpretation of Biblical tradition out of step with most twentieth century thinking, including religious philosophy. In his poetry, however, Jacob succeeds in imposing his vision of the supernatural by making it appear a completely ordinary, even commonplace dimension of reality, as in the following poem, quoted in its entirety:

> L'archange foudroyé n'eut que le temps de desserrer sa cravate, on aurait dit qu'il priait encore.
> (Untitled, CD, p. 57).

A number of images are superimposed: the gesture of unknotting one's tie, the position of one who is praying, and the attitude of a man who is falling after being mortally wounded. The archangel has been thunderstruck so suddenly that he is caught performing a familiar act. The poem, through its emphasis, succeeds in making the supernatural seem completely normal. The focus on the position of the archangel implies that the only unusual event is his being struck by a thunderbolt. To the poet, his presence requires no further comment, nor does his modern dress.

Similarly, the devil is a ubiquitous presence in Jacob's poetry, masquerading under the most innocuous guises, but always corporally, physically present. The image in the line "Il paraît que les diables vinrent en personnes," from "Petit Essai sur le diable," CD, II, p. 52, while humorous, must be interpreted literally. Consider also the following images:

> C'est une petite fille méchante: son profil est pointu comme ses dents et sa couronne.
> ("Mystique noire," CD, II, p. 47);

> Il y eut un rire dans les boiseries quand le vieux député dit que sa vie était finie.
> ("Le Monde est au diable," VI, p. 79).

In the first image, the profile of the young girl is a caricature of the conventional profile of Satan: she is literally possessed, as the title indicates. In the second image, the laughter is literally that of the devil, claiming his prey. Laughter, in Jacob's poetry, is nearly always threatening: e.g.: "que dire des rires?" in "L'Enfer est gradué," VI, p. 32, which is given as the first of a series of details characterizing hell.

Again, similar effects can be achieved uniquely through structural patterns. Thus, in

> Chaque fleur de papier a du sang sur les ailes, chaque animal a du sang sur les pétales...
> ("Voisinage," VI, p. 55)

the interversion of *ailes* and *pétales* (in addition to the image of "sang") creates the oneiric dimension. An even simpler inversion may accomplish the same purpose:

> ...les bandits sont des soldats...
> ("La Guerre," CD, p. 24).

A similar effect can result from the removal of a familiar object to an incongruous setting:

> Cette nuit-là, la Seine coulait à Londres.
> ("Nocturne," CD, II, p. 49).

An image may have oneiric overtones without being explicit. In

> Rue Ordener, l'horreur grandissait.
> (Untitled, SM, p. 276),

horreur, an abstract noun, is concretised by being preceded by the definite article and followed by a verb of action. The specific location of the image, the name of a street in Paris, again makes the abnormal seem commonplace. A similar effect may be obtained through the use of indefinite words:

> Quelque chose d'horriblement froid tombe sur mes épaules. Quelque chose de gluant s'attache à mon cou.
> ("Nuit infernale," CD, p. 73).

The generally weak *quelque chose* becomes nightmarish because of the adjectives "d'horriblement froid" and "gluant" that turn it into a loathsome, unnameable thing.

Some more highly developed oneiric images constitute comparisons which are not made explicit. An example is "Incendie," CD, II, p. 102:

> C'est le feu! le feu! les pompiers: on se sauve! Or dans la foule paraît, accompagnée de son époux en habit, la plus belle, la plus grande mariée du monde. Auréole de satin blanc, flamme et fumée.

This image of the bride appearing among the flames accompanied by a bridegroom in evening clothes is not explicitly oneiric, but the renewal of the clichés, *la plus belle, la plus grande*, here developed literally, implying both disproportionate size and unreal beauty, turns it into an oneiric image. The poem establishes an implicit relationship between the smoke, the flames, and the bride. This comparison is established only in the final image: "Auréole de satin blanc, flamme et fumée" where the bride's veils, the smoke, and the flames become one.

Oneiric images constitute the basis for many short poems. For example:

> Des sabots pour dames! nous les faisons en drap de soldats morts. Par les découpures brodées le sang coule en cas de blessures et ça fait piste sur la neige.
>
> (Untitled, DP, p. 194).

The poem occurs in a section of short poems entitled "Folklore, 1943," which constitute brief characterizations of that year. It creates an incongruous link between the scarcity engendered by the war and the prevalence of death, and it juxtaposes other incongruities as well. It is written in the style either of an advertisement or a recipe, which causes its macabre aspects to appear even more sinister. The images of the blood of dead soldiers flowing from sheets or shoes (a mutilation characteristic of oneiric images), as well as that of the red blood against the white snow, all suggest death. The contrast between "sabots pour dames" and "découpures brodées" underlines further the oneiric quality of the images.

Longer poems are also based on oneiric themes chiefly voyages into the unknown which become voyages towards death. These themes, as Bachelard has shown, are archetypal. In Jacob's poetry, however, the voyages occur in a setting where the familiar becomes the unknown, the threatening world: the supernatural and the oneiric are physically there, a part of the "real," the daily world. In "L'Enfer est gradué," VI, p. 32, for example, a descent into a basement turns into a descent into hell. In "Séjour," VI, p. 53, the passengers aboard a ship suddenly all become repellent monsters: again, the ship is bound for hell. In "La Guerre," CD, p. 24, a familiar winter city scene is the setting for a nightmare dream embodying the theme of pursuit and attack:

> Les boulevards extérieurs, la nuit, sont pleins de neige; les bandits sont des soldats; on m'attaque avec des rires et des sabres, on me dépouille: je me sauve pour retomber dans un autre carré. Est-ce une cour de caserne, ou celle d'une auberge? que de sabres! que de lanciers! il neige! on me pique avec une seringue: c'est un poison pour me tuer; une tête de squelette voilée de crêpe me mord le doigt. De vagues réverbères jettent sur la neige la lumière de ma mort.

The title of this poem links it to others with similar titles; for example, "1914" in CD, II, pp. 21 and 23, as well as "Aout 39," in CD, II, p. 150. A number of images are oneiric: "les bandits sont des soldats," (previously cited); "On me pique avec une seringue: c'est un poison pour me tuer; . . ." and "Une tête de squelette voilée de crêpe de mord le doigt," both of which are death images and images of hell that embody the sinister mutilation of objects. Other elements in the poem reinforce their affective impact: the use of words such as "neige," "nuit," "mort," which in this context underline the death theme; the exclamations translating fear; the repetition of "il neige!" (snow and death are so often associated with each other in world literature as to constitute an archetypal theme). Two images other than these oneiric ones are particularly striking: "on m'attaque avec des rires et des sabres" in which "rire" by being juxtaposed with "attack" and "sabers" becomes a concretised, sinister weapon; and the final image: "De vagues réverbères jettent sur la neige la lumière de ma mort," in which the adjective "vagues" gives the lampposts the unreality of objects in a dream, and the phrase "lumière de ma mort" concretises death in an abstract metaphor.

Among innumerable poems with the same theme, one in particular stands out:

> On vient nous arrêter!... mes amis sont assis sur le billard: moi, je reboutonne ma veste cachant lá-dessous des papiers, de l'encre: n'oublions pas l'encre de Chine, c'est pour mes dessins...
>
> (Untitled, SM, p. 273).

The theme of this poem, that of pursuit and arrest, is oneiric, even though its images, as well as its tone — the calm and methodical preparations of the speaker for his arrest — do not suggest that anything is happening beyond the normal, the expected. This appearance of "business as usual" is the cause of the particularly sinister impact of the poem, which corresponds not only to the fears of a specific individual, but to those of an age: the knock on the door heralding arrest, whether by the Gestapo or the secret police.

Related to this recurrent theme of attack and murder is the theme of transformation involving the loss of identity:

> Je fuis à travers les fleurs aussi innombrables que des herbes et, quand je veux cueillir le jasmin sauvage, c'est un arbre que je secoue et il est mort.
>
> ("Péché dans la recherche de la vertu," DT, p. 146).

Changing a flower into a tree that dies constitutes an oneiric transformation, evidently a death image. "Jasmine" has no particular significance beyond its role in the transformation theme; however, the choice of vocabulary (e. g. the flowers, the theme of flight), the shock of the final image, the syntax (the successive disjunctions which create suspense), all turn this image into a particularly lyrical one. The title of the poem suggests, in addition, that the oneiric image is a parable whose significance is made explicit by the final sentence: "Mon père, secourez-moi!" The death image and transformation represent the symbolic death (or lack of human ability) that occurs without the grace of God. The oneiric content of a poem like this one, with its strong emotional impact, turns it into a particularly effective vehicle for a parable, since the message of the parable is reinforced by the affective qualities of the poem.

Oneiric poems need not be interpreted on one level only. In "Temps de révolution," CD, II, p. 133, a scene is given which may be interpreted in ordinary terms, yet, as is usual in Jacob's poetry, possesses disturbing overtones:

> Désert est le pavé de bois, noir est le pavé de bois de la rue de Sèvres. Des camions dételés le long des immeubles aux volets clos. Quel étrange dimanche! Une infirmière traverse en regardant s'il va pleuvoir, et moi, je cours quelque part. Un jeune homme déclame: "On fait des kilomètres pour placer ses écrits, des kilomètres à pied! pour manger..." Et sa voix retentit dans le vide solennel. Ce dont il faut se méfier surtout c'est des faux mendiants.

The details given need not have sinister implications: the emptiness of the street, the unloaded trucks, the closed shutters, all of these are usual for early Sunday mornings. The complaint of the young man might very well have been that of any *littérateur*, including Max Jacob himself, in normal times. The title, however, as well as such words as "désert," "noir," "étrange," and in this context, "quelque part," create an atmosphere of unreality or abnormality. The inversions of the first sentence, emphasizing "désert" and "noir," underline this effect. Even the final comment, which could be merely a cliché of conversation, or the words of an eccentric, acquires sinister implications. The title can be interpreted literally or figuratively; the reality depicted, as an evocation of revolutionary times, or as a nightmare.

This effect is compatible with humor as in this excerpt from "Voyages," in CD, p. 121:

> Jamais je n'en sortirai: je cours dire au revoir à ma tante, je trouve la famille sous la lampe; on me retient pour mille recommandations, ma valise est faite, mais mon complet est encore chez le teinturier: j'ai de la peine à reconnaître mon costume: ce n'est pas mon costume, on l'a changé! non, c'est lui, mais affreusement gonflé, mutilé, tiré, recousu, bordé de noir. Dehors, dans la rue, deux délicieuses Bretonnes rient près d'une charrette de linge: que n'ai-je le temps de les suivre; bah! elles prennent dans la nuit le même chemin que moi.

On one level, the poem tells a humorous anecdote: the cliché "Jamais je n'en sortirai" is interpreted literally and expanded with copious details. The structure of the first sentence, a series of added-on phrases, each of which adds a new, unanticipated detail, is mimetic of the bewilderment of the "I." Everything seems to happen to him at once; he is overwhelmed by the multiplicity of things he must do. As the poem progresses, however, the cliché "Jamais je n'en sortirai" is given a second interpretation: the voyage becomes the final journey into the unknown. With "non, c'est lui, mais affreusement gonflé, mutilé, tiré, recousu, bordé de noir," the theme of mutilation and death becomes explicit: the suit appears, not merely mauled by a careless cleaner, but it takes on the hideous quality of a bloated cadaver. The significance of the "charrette de linge" and the "Bretonnes" is equally ambiguous: they could be what they seem, literally; their laughter, however, as well as their following the traveler into the night, suggests that they are meant as death images. With "elles prennent dans la nuit le même chemin que moi...." the theme of the journey towards death becomes inescapable. The literal meaning of the poem, as a caricatural anecdote concerning a befuddled man, continues to subsist, however, along with the more sinister death theme.

In other poems, both the oneiric and the comic dimensions are more caricatural, more exaggerated. One bewildered soul, in "Poème," (CD, p. 44) exclaims: "Et moi, je n'ai plus de relations pour retrouver des places! Formulaires! Formulaires! il y a un nombre constant qui est 2.241, par lequel il faut multiplier les autres... En repassant, j'irai chez la blanchisseuse, cette personne qui me rend des bas de femme pour mes chaussettes et des bas percés de *mille trous*." (Italics mine). In both of these texts, the choice of details creates a superimposition of meanings. Each image, because of the others, can be read on any of the levels mentioned. Each becomes a complex sign, embodying the complexity of reality, the overlapping of worlds, which is typical of the kabbalistic vision of the world. The subtitle of one of Jacob's poems: "Poème mystique" (from "Roman Policier, in CD, II, p. 155) is valid for the preceding poems and the type of interpretation explicitly stated in that text: "C'est un simple roman policier... Je soutiens que c'est une parabole. Le diamant est la

Sainte Hostie..." applies, even when not explicitly stated. Philosophy is then, in Jacob's phrase of Conseils à un jeune poète, p. 21: "incluse et invisible."

Figurative imagery: simile.

Figurative imagery is as old as literature. When the reader thinks of imagery, he probably thinks of figurative imagery, especially simile, and metaphor. Simile is the expanded version of metaphor; it establishes an explicit analogy between two objects, as in "He is as courageous as a lion," the simplest example, structurally, of a simile.[7] Simile is often treated as a watered down version of metaphor, less original, or less strong in its effect on the reader. This generality is not justified, however, since the very explicitness of the simile permits bold analogies. Moreover, there can be more than one point of comparison between the two terms of a simile, so that it can achieve considerable complexity.

Jacob's similes are characterized, first of all, by great boldness, assimilating widely removed contexts. Twentieth century theoreticians of poetry have particularly emphasized that the more removed the two terms of an image are from each other, the greater the force of the image. The resulting surprise allows even simple similes such as "Un cœur d'adolescent gardé comme une amphore..." ("Vers sans art," DP, p. 72), to acquire great force. This comparison is based both on an analogy of forms, the shape of the heart being compared to that of the amphora, and on an analogy of value: the "cœur d'adolescent" has been watched with the infinite care usually bestowed on a treasured, fragile, and beautiful object. The traditional theme of the value of youth is renewed by this formulation into an image that is both affective and expressive.

Few similes in Jacob's poetry however, conform to this simple structural pattern. Jacob generally expands the expressiveness or affective value of a simile by modifying its basic structural pattern. His modifications represent two divergent tendencies. The first is toward density. The simile is divested of some or most of

---

[7] Both the term "simple" and the example are those of Michael Riffaterre, *Le Style des Pléiades de Gobineau,* op. cit., p. 172.

the explicit links that distinguish it from metaphor. The other tendency is towards expansion. The simile is developed by being immediately followed by a tableau or a metaphor, or it may develop a metaphor.

The elimination of one or more of the explicit links that distinguish a simile from a metaphor permits a direct confrontation of the two terms of the simile. An analogy can be made explicit through a verb, although this is, of necessity, comparatively rare and is limited to such verbs as "to be," "to resemble," or the like (use of any different type of verb, of motion or action, for example, would by definition result in a metaphor):

> Son pantalon est si long qu'il fait le tire-bouchon vers les souliers.
> ("Méli-mélo," CD, p. 190);

> ... ... il était de Bretagne,
> pays qui tient du prêtre et du tzigane!
> ("La Vraie Jeunesse," DP, p. 38).

The relative weakness or colorlessness of the verbs "est" and "tient" gives greatest prominence to the second term of the simile. In the first example, the emphasis on "tire-bouchon" results in a humorous and sharp visual image; in the second, the juxtaposition of "prêtre" and "tzigane," of the religious (or superstitious) with the charlatan, emphasizes those aspects of Brittany. In a variation of the preceding example, the analogy is made explicit through the verb "to be," but in the conditional mood, as in the following example:

> Si les pruneaux étaient couleur d'olive claire
> Ce seraient des pruneaux que ces vieillards sévères,
> ("Honneur de la sardane et de la ténora," LC, p. 49).

This form permits the juxtaposition of more than two terms in a simile. The analogy superimposes three visual images: the wrinkled faces of old Spanish men, the color of light olives, and the wrinkled appearance of prunes. The image is humorous, but the meaning of "sévères" and "claire" adds a note both of light-heartedness and dignity.

The potential towards multiplication of the terms of the simile is even more fully realized in another stanza of the same poem (p. 53) in which the accumulation of a series of five analogies, made explicit through the verb "to be," again in the conditional, results in a dynamic evocation of the movement of the dance:

> Le peuple serait comme les vagues de la mer
> Si la mer était rose et tournait dans la nuit,
> Si la nuit était rose, si rose était la mer
> Et si la mer était comme les arbres verts.

This stanza occurs directly after a description of the dance named in the title, the "sardane" (p. 52):

> Au centre de la ronde, il y a une autre ronde et au milieu de cette ronde, une autre; et les mouvements de ces rondes sont les mêmes, mais ne coincident pas, parce que chaque meneur de ronde n'a pas le même sentiment de la musique.

Jacob then compares the figure formed by the circles of dancers to a rose, adding that most of the young ladies are wearing the color "rose." In the stanza under consideration, a third image, that of the movement of waves on the sea, is superimposed upon the other two: that of the circles of dancers in motion, and that of a rose. Either meaning of rose, as color or flower, is applicable to each use of the term, in each of the segments of the simile. The rhythm resulting from the visual imagery, the syntax (the repetition of "si" clauses), and the repeated pun (suggesting an endless succession and confusion of motion and meaning) becomes mimetic of the movement of the dance and of the general configurations of the dancers.

Frequently, an analogy is made explicit through an adjectival phrase:

> Et par-dessus les bras tendus en candélabres!
> ("Honneur de la sardane et de la ténora," LC, p. 53);
>
> une nuit de douce mère...
> ("Présence de Dieu," DP, p. 93).

The use of an adjectival phrase permits a direct confrontation of the two terms of the comparison. The first example results in a visual analogy, comparing the position of the Spanish dancers to the shape of a candelabrum. The second example is more complex. The use of the adjectival phrase concretizes the qualities inherent in reminiscences of "gentle" and "sweet mother," transforming them into a material substance, into the very stuff that makes up the night. Moreover *douce-mère* suggests a pun on *dure-mère* (dura-mater), the strong outer membrane of the brain, which emphasizes the mother's protective qualities of strength. Since the context of this simile is a poem based on the analogy, traditional in mystical poetry, between the embrace of a lover and the presence of God (cf. the title), it suggests erotic connotations as well.

Any linking words are often eliminated altogether, and the terms compared to each other are juxtaposed without any transition. Two or more series of terms may be so juxtaposed:

Le danseur: — un zeste de citron —
("Thème de l'illusion et de l'amour," LC, p. 135);

Un pan de ciel bleu, un peu de fumée comme un duvet de cygne: des anges en voyage.
(Untitled, CD, p. 66).

The second quotation constitutes an entire poem, untitled. This form of ellipsis is by definition dense. But more importantly, the direct confrontation of terms in each instance creates a rapport of identity between them. The result is mid-way between metaphor and comparison. Each term is placed on an equal footing with the other, given equal prominence since either term is interchangeable with the other: the dancer is a "zeste de citron" and vice versa. In the second example, the theme is the familiar one of the ubiquitous presence of the supernatural. The comparison between the puffs of smoke and angel's wings is brought about very naturally through the intervening comparison between the puffs of smoke and the down of swan's wings. The lack of explicit connectives expands the possibilities of the simile in that, since all terms are equally important, the comparison applies either to puffs of smoke or to angel's wings. The image can also be interpreted literally, as if one could look up on a nice day and expect to see real angels flying by. The colors, moreover, suggest a very clear day and a world of innocence and prettiness, in which the presence of angels does not need to be justified.

Related to the above is a comparison in which the elliptical juxtaposition of images is, so to speak, inverted: the second term of the comparison reveals that an object is not what the reader thought it was, but something else:

> J'ai trois fausses fenêtres d'ivoire sous la cigarette:
> j'ai trois dents fausses.
> ("Conscience," CD, II, p. 174).

This form of the comparison poses a kind of riddle, which strengthens its potential for surprise. Here the comic surprise results from the assimilation of false teeth to ivory windows. In other poems the surprise may be more lyrical, as in the following:

> Un buisson d'épines bleu pâle, c'est un clocher dans le clair de lune.
> (Untitled, CD, p. 54);

> Il y a dans ma chambre obscure une navette lumineuse qui rôde, puis deux... des aérostats phosphorescents, c'est les reflets d'un miroir.
> ("Poème de la lune," CD, p. 71).

The first example again constitutes an entire poem. In each case, the setting (the night), and the moonlight, justify the optical illusions and the tricks of the imagination. Each of these similes renews concretely, through visual images, the clichés associated with night and moonlight.

Similes made explicit through conventional links, e.g. "he is as courageous as a lion," generally occur within a larger sequence of imagery. They can occur immediately after an abstract metaphor, which is concretized and developed by the simile:

> Mes désirs de Dieu s'élèvent, se dilatent
> Comme une voile blanche en un jour de Régates
> ("Les Yeux au ventre," FddL, n. p.);

La colère de Dieu s'étend comme un hamac
    ("Corpus Christi," FddL, n. p.);

La verdure était souriante comme au matin de l'Angélus
    ("La Vraie Jeunesse," DP, p. 39);

La musique a gelé dans l'air froid
comme une vérité céleste:
    ("Esprit de Raymond Radiguet," FddL, n. p.).

In the first example, "s'élèvent, se dilatent," constitute almost fossilized metaphors, clichés. *Se dilater* in particular is frequently used in the religious vocabulary. Jacob's simile gives new life to the clichés. "Comme une voile blanche" illustrates visually, and therefore concretely, the concept of expansion that is abstract in the verbs "se dilatent" and "s'élèvent." "Régates" expands the affective connotations of the image by bringing to mind the secondary connotations associated with Regattas: a clear day, the blue sea, excitement, joy "S'étend," in the second example, is a pallid metaphor. The image concretizes through visual analogy. The choice of the vehicle for the comparison, however, the "hamac" (the term vehicle, introduced by I. A. Richards, designates the literal meaning of an image), gives great force to the metaphor by linking two widely removed contexts: the divine and the mundane. There is, in addition, an interpenetration of the various terms of the simile: the hammock assumes giant proportions while God's wrath spreads like a tangible presence. In example number three, the personification of nature resulting from the use of "souriante," an affective metaphor, is given further affective connotations by the analogy with a morning prayer. This comparison is less direct than the preceding two, since it is, based on an analogy between states of mind or emotion rather than concrete sensuous representation. The final example is the most abstract of all, and hence the most surprising, since both the metaphor of the first line and the simile of the second are concretizations of abstractions: the juxtaposition of "gelé," "air froid," and "musique" suggests visual analogies by bringing to mind suspended particles of frost, analogous to the representation of musical notes suspended on a musical staff.

The comparison with "vérité céleste" suggests further that the presence of these images is as permanent as are celestial truths.

A simile sometimes follows not one, but a series of metaphors, prolonging or crystallizing their various suggestions:

> Anonyme, tu as usé de la lumière
> Reporte à Dieu ton loyer éphémère
> Comme la vague à l'océan.
> ("Acte de reconnaissance," HdC, p. 152).

"Lumière" is used figuratively to indicate the light of day, or of life. The figurative meaning of "loyer" derives from two of its meanings: its literal sense as rent; its figurative moral sense (such expressions as "the wages of sin"). The final comparison derives from poetic diction. The theme of this series of images is a conventional one in lyric poetry: the brevity of life, the littleness of man, and the presence of death. Yet this series of images is a complex and very expressive one. Each succeeding image juxtaposes contexts on totally different time scales, through antithesis. The first line evokes the littleness of man (through "anonyme") and the universality of light; the second, the presence of God, the trivia of daily existence (rent), and through the moral sense of *loyer*, the payment, either judgment or death, due to the Deity. The final comparison is extremely complex in its associations. It has the effect of bringing to the fore the many connotations evoked by the sea; and more specifically, the analogy between the rythms of life and those of the sea, the ritual grandeur of one of the most basic cycles of existence, human life and death as a natural part of these patterns. The comparison achieves both grandeur and serenity, since dying, giving one's life into God's hands, is made to seem as simple an act as paying one's rent; as natural as the tides of the sea; as grandiose as its rhythms. This image reformulates strikingly a perpetual lyrical theme.

A simile can also be followed by a tableau. This tableau permits the author to expand the meaning of the comparison as much or as little as he wishes, through the number of details supplied. In

> J'ai longtemps cru la vie comme un brouillard d'automne
> fait de lacs éloignés coupés de sables ocreux
> fait de branches séchées, de buissons monotones
>
> ("Vers sans art," DP, p. 72),

the comparison between life and the autumn fog is primarily affective, in the realm of what Baudelaire would have called "correspondances," evoking the melancholy mood of autumn, haziness. The visual images of the tableau that follow this simile provide a symbolic *décor* that prolongs the suggestions of hopelessness, lifelessness, monotony. There is not a one-to-one correspondance between the additional detail supplied and the initial comparison. Rather, the entire tableau suggests a mood which is the affective equivalent of the visual images.

A tableau illustrating a simile can develop into an entire poem, such as the following, entitled "La France," dated January 11, 1942, in CD, II, p. 169:

> La douleur vous sort comme un eczéma et les émigrés ont un volcan épiderme; ça leur a pourri les dents; l'estomac est presque une échancrure qui descend aux ongles pour les soutacher de lèpres. Léproserie! La route d'eau sous les peupliers est une léproserie en marche. La léproserie ne marche pas vers la mer, elle se dévore l'estomac comme un bigorneau et il en sort l'eczéma, le psoriasis et l'érésipèle.... Un jour, le tonnerre fend la saumure, l'arc-en-ciel ou moitié [sic] a ressuscité les cerisiers en fleurs: ils sont pourris.

I have omitted a section of the poem, but the quotation suffices to illustrate its technique. The initial simile is an extremely bold one because the repulsive qualities of *eczéma* become all the more shocking since poetic grief is usually associated with nobility and beauty. The force of the comparison derives precisely from its shock value. The continued accumulation of similarly repulsive details — primarily diseases characterized by decay of the skin — expresses both affectively and symbolically the physical and moral rottenness of France in 1942. Its successive metaphorical personifications as a vast leprosarium, a self-devouring mollusc *(bigorneau)*, can also be interpreted as parables. Only two details relieve the ambiance of rottenness of the poem: the allusions in the final sentence to a rainbow and to cherry trees in bloom. Yet they are evoked only because they too, have been destroyed by the all-enveloping disease. The poem seems perverse in its relentless evocation of decay; but the almost physical repulsion is an appropriate response to the subject of the poem, the moral decay of France in 1942. The use of such shocking imagery is therefore effective, and justified.

Metaphor.

Metaphor is formally defined as a condensed form of the simile. The linking words that make an analogy explicit disappear. Either a relationship of identity is posited between two objects through the use of the verb "to be" (a is b); or the term of the comparison is substituted for the object to which it is being compared. In twentieth century criticism, metaphor is regarded as the central figure in poetry. The effort to properly analyse the role of metaphor in poetry had led critics to regard the formal definition of metaphor as insufficient. Max Black and Hedwig Konrad, notably, have pointed out that if metaphor is classified primarily as a figure of analogy, its value becomes merely ornamental, metaphor merely expressing a thought more forcefully, or more elegantly, than another figure of speech.[8] They have argued that metaphor, which is not a uniquely literary phenomenon, represents a genuine method of investigation through which the unknown is assimilated to the known, and they have argued that in literature as in science, the chief function of metaphor is the extension of meaning which accrues to any word or phrase used metaphorically. They would like to replace the formal definition of metaphor which stresses structure with one stressing its semantic function of expressing a wholly self-contained idea through a concrete image.

Each of these definitions represents a possible pole. One emphasizes structure; the other, semantic function. The first would label as metaphors all those images that conform to the formal definition. The latter would expand the term to include any image

---

[8] See Hedwig Konrad, *Etude sur la métaphore* (Paris, 1958), pp. 106-130 and Max Black, *Models and Metaphors* (Cornell University Press), pp. 12-46.

that fulfills the semantic function ascribed to metaphor. There is considerable overlap since many metaphors that conform to the formal definition also meet the requirements of the semantic. The images that I have selected for analysis satisfy both definitions. Moreover, the functional criterion may help in evaluating a metaphor: the more nearly it approaches the norm of expressing a self-contained idea through a concrete image, the more force it possesses. Similarly, this functional definition provides a ready explanation for the element of surprise generated by metaphor since, with the exclusion of fossilized metaphors whose metaphorical origin has been forgotten, any metaphorical image always uses a word in a new and therefore unexpected way. The total impact the metaphor has on the reader may be viewed as the result of an interplay of factors: its surprise value, the concretizing effect of the image, the associations the selected image may provoke, and the extent to which it succeeds in assimilating the known to the unknown.

Metaphor, unhampered by any need for explicit links, can appear in unlimited structural variations. A metaphor can be extremely condensed (one word used metaphorically), or it can be developed, becoming an autonomous syntactical structure or even a poem.

Any word or section of a sentence may be used metaphorically, with a variety of results. A verb used metaphorically results in a dynamic image in

>Des étoiles grouillaient comme un boisseau d'abeilles
>("Plus d'Astrologie," LC, p. 115).

Grouiller, which means "to swarm," constitutes a metaphorical personification that gives intense life to a night sky. The metaphor, in addition, is completed by a visual comparison that underlines both the movement and the scintillation of the stars.

A noun used metaphorically may suggest more than one interpretation, as in

>Avril avec ses catafalques
>de tulipiers...
>("Enterrement à Quimper," DP, p. 53).

The "catafalques" of flowers suggest a double visual image: the flowers are associated with a funeral or with the abundant bloom of April. In addition, the word "catafalques" evokes the theme of death. Its association with April suggests that nature herself is mourning, that the flowers are blooming as a symbol not of life, but of death.

Brief metaphors, like similes or lengthier metaphors, can renew fossilized metaphors through a process analogous to the renewal of a cliché, as in:

> Il admirait votre sourire perlier.
> (Untitled, LC, p. 183).

Teeth in poetry are commonly called pearls. Here, the adjective *perlier*, as an attribute of the smile, suggests the teeth revealed by the smile, and hence, its brightness. The unaccustomed preciosity of the image causes it to appear somewhat humorous.

Expanded metaphors in Jacob's poetry belong to two groups: those that develop one central image, and series of metaphors that succeed each other in a somewhat looser relationship. Metaphors developing one central image constitute metaphorical tableaux. One type evokes some aspect of the environment:

> Le ciel a pour la mer des regards qui bénissent
> Le soleil sur la mer est un bateau qui glisse
> Chaque lame a son or, chaque écume a sa nuit
> Le flot donne un mot d'ordre à la vague qui suit
> ("Cancale, le crépuscule," LC, p. 85).

Cancale is the name of a small island, off St. Malo, in Brittany. The title indicates the subject of the poem, twilight (probably sunset, but the evocation could apply equally to a sunrise) at the island of Cancale. The entire poem (which continues in the same vein as the beginning, quoted above) constitutes a metaphorical description of twilight, which is developed through a series of individual images that single out an aspect of the sunset for personification. The image is neither obscure nor particularly original, since sunsets at sea have been perennial subjects of poetry. Yet it is nevertheless effective on a number of levels. The personification is dynamic. In addition, the last two lines cited translate an impression of universal harmony: the sunset develops along the lines of a well organized ritual in which each element plays a pre-ordained role. The choice of vocabulary ("bénissent," for example) reinforces affectively this impression of peace and tranquillity, so that the description is interpretable symbolically as an outer manifestation of a universal order. This type of symbolism can be more explicit. For example, "La Nuit," in FfdL, n. p., begins with these lines:

> Troupeau, abondant troupeau des astres
> Tant d'ordre et de lenteur pour quelle cérémonie?

The interrogation, the words "cérémonie" and "ordre" imply a predetermined ritual: the entire heavens become a metaphor, revealing an ordering intelligence.

Jacob's developed metaphors, unlike the preceding two, generally tend towards myth or vision. The simplest structure of this type consists of a metaphor concretized by a tableau which follows it:

> La terre est une grande bouche souillée
> ses hoquets, ses rires à gorge déployée
> sa toux, son haleine, ses ronflements quand elle dort
> me triturent l'âme...
> ("La Terre," SI, in MC, p. 101).

The metaphor "la terre est une grande bouche souillée" personifies the earth and, by implication, life, as the mouth of a soiled (morally unclean) person. The image is visionary or even hallucinatory since the equation between the earth and a mouth causes the mouth to appear monstrous. The subsequent tableau shares this disproportion. More importantly, it personifies the earth as a woman whose coughs, too loud laughs, bad breath, and snores are not merely unpleasant, but which, given the phrase "me triturent l'âme" (*triturent* means both to crush and to torture) are the sources of the torment of the I, and morally annihilate his soul. There is not a one-to-one correspondance between the details of this image, and the reality it suggests. Rather, the entire image, that is, the initial metaphor plus the tableau following it, has affective and semantic value, portraying concretely the horror of the speaker for earthly existence and making it clear that it is the physical aspects of existence which disgust him. In a similar manner, the simile analysed on page 120: "J'ai longtemps cru la vie comme un brouillard d'automne..." i. e. the initial comparison plus the tableau which follows it, constitute a physical description (desolate desert, autumn fog) which is a metaphorical evocation of a state of mind. Similarly (also in "La Terre," SI, in MC, p. 101) a sensual metaphorical description concretises an unknowable reality:

> Surnaturel, je me cramponne à ton drapeau de soie
> Que le grand vent me coule dans tes plis qui ondoient!

In this apostrophe, the silken emblem constitutes a metaphorical (metonymic) evocation of the supernatural. Once again, the metaphor is primarily affective: the syntax (the exclamations), the vocabulary (e. g. *cramponne,* to cling, suggesting the gesture of a frightened child clinging for protection), as well as the tactile and visual sensations evoked (the silken emblem, the wind, their freshness and prettiness), all suggest various emotions: the need of the speaker for protection, his appeal and faith in a higher power, and the like.

Similar but more extended metaphors take the form of a personification that develops a dramatic, although imaginary (metaphorical) anecdote:

> Hors! ça! enfuyez-vous, noirceurs
> qui souillez tout jusqu'à mon cœur
> ("Taie divine," DP, p. 74).

> Sur les remparts d'Edimbourg
> tant de douleur se marie
> ce soir
> avec tant d'amour
> que ton cheval Poésie
> en porte une voile noire
> ("Angoisses et autres," FddL, n. p.).

In the first example, the speaker is trying to exorcise the monsters that bedevil him, personified by the substantive "noirceurs." Again, the metaphor is primarily affective. The exclamation translates emotion; the vocabulary, especially "souillez" expresses moral repugnance; "cœur" is used metonymically for emotion, but opposed to "souillez," it takes on the additional connotation of pure emotion, correct instincts. The figures evoked in the second example are allegorical personifications. The name *Edimbourg* was probably chosen for its euphonic value, to repeat the "ou" sound of "amour" and "douleur." This use of allegorical imagery differs from traditional allegory in that there is no obvious application. The various personages of the allegory ("douleur," "amour," "Poésie," the "cheval") do not represent anything other than themselves. They evolve in a kind of ballet, vaguely reminiscent (though the allusions to "remparts," "cheval," the "voile noire" emblematic of sorrow) of medieval pageantry. The metaphorical *récit* or allegory is both concrete and dynamic. The preceding stanzas of the poem oppose sacred and profane love, evoking the torment that his divided allegiances cause the speaker. The stanza prolongs the affective overtones of the preceding stanzas, partly through the allegorical personifications of "douleur," "amour," and the image of the "voile noire," and partly through the associations evoked by such images as "voile noire" (death, defeat), "remparts" (fortress, retreat or attack), "soir" (the poetic time for sorrow and sin). This stanza, which concludes the poem, does not reconcile the opposition of the two loves. Rather, it holds the multiple associations of the poem together in one poetic image which contains all the contradictory postulations of the lyrical I.

The most striking instance of this type of development occurs when a dramatic personification takes the form of a quasi mythological *récit*. The following is representative:

> Je partirai demain pour d'éternelles vacances!
> Toute la nuit, j'ai vu les bêtes du printemps
> Et toute la nuit, j'ai reçu les confidences
> Des sirènes de l'air et du nain Marmotan
>
> Ah! laissez-moi passer, vous, chasseurs de ménades
> Les seigneurs des saules d'argent
> Maintenant j'ai dégonflé les Titans mages
> Et retrouvé les mères aux fleuves de légendes

....
....
....
....

....
....
Moi! la mort est ma sœur, les saints peuvent m'attendre
Car Cybèle n'a plus de geôle pour ma peau
            ("La Mort," HdC, p. 159).

The central metaphor developed by this enumeration of images is the familiar one of a voyage into the unknown, here towards death, designated by the periphrasis of the first line as "des éternelles vacances," which makes it clear that, for the speaker, death represents a joyful departure. A secondary theme, developed through allusion, hints at a combat of the lyrical I with mysterious forces, personified as mythological figures, which preceded this departure. The triumph of the I over these malevolent forces is the source of his confidence in looking forward to death. The most explicit allusions are to figures that participate in various existing systems of myth: Cybèle (Greek mythology) and the saints (Christian mythology). The allusion to Cybèle is particularly significant since she was not only the goddess of the earth, but also a figure worshipped by sodomists, and particularly, by homosexuals.[9] In the light of this, the lines: "les saints peuvent m'attendre / car Cybèle n'a plus de grêle pour ma peau..." indicate that the I has triumphed over his carnal homosexual desires. The allusions to a fight with the "demons of spring," the fact that the combat took place at night, retroactively strengthen these implications.

Too much emphasis on the explicitness of these allusions, however, obscures the fact that other references are veiled,

---

[9] See Robert Graves, *The Greek Myths* (Penguin Books, 1959), I, p. 71 and 117. Cybèle was the nymph goddess who destroyed her mate, the sacred king, in midsummer by tearing out his sexual organs. Her priests immolated themeslves by self-castration. In Greece, worship of Cybèle provided justification for the passionate love of a grown man for a boy; her priests tried to achieve ecstatic unity with Cybèle by emasculating themselves and dessing like women.

couched in terms which keep a precise interpretation at bay. A number of these are to figure which suggest but do not participate in any specific system of myth. "Les sirènes de l'air" cannot be identified with Greek sirens since the latter dwell in the water. "Les seigneurs des saules d'argent" represent woodland deities of no particular provenance. The name of the dwarf Marmotan is coined by Jacob. The "chasseurs de ménades" probably represent a generalized allusion to any forces which hound those who hound poets. A number of the mythological figures of the poem constitute entirely metaphorical creations: "les Titans mages" and "les mères aux fleuves des légendes," a personification which piles metaphor upon metaphor since the mothers are metaphorical and the rivers are figurative. The meaning of this phrase, in this context of myth, might be either "the mother figures of all legends" or the "primary (fundamental) mythical figures at the origin of legends." Moreover, words such as "mother" and "rivers," as Bachelard has shown, have extraordinary suggestive power.[10] In a context of myth, where death is both the goal and the sister, they assume singular dimensions.

The reader may not be familiar with this particular cycle of the Cybèle myth, and he may thus miss some of the suggestions to which this allusion points. Moreover, the mythical figures to which the poem alludes have different origins. Both of these facts, however, are irrelevant since what is of importance is not so much the precise meaning of each mythical allusion, but the fact that it is perceived as myth. Each mythical allusion makes it clear that the "I" of the poem is engaged in a kind of combat. Each represents mysterious forces which he must conquer before achieving a safe passage towards death. Thus, the metaphor is extremely powerful, partly because it turns death into a joyful departure, but mainly because by pitting the "I" against mythical or legendary figures, the author endows him also with legendary dimensions: the combat of the "I," his triumph over malevolent forces, take on the dimensions of myth.

Occasionally, quasi-mythical figures are used entirely for purposes of fantasy or humor, as in the following excerpt:

---

[10] See for example, *L'Eau et les rêves* (Paris, 1941).

> Je danse en rond avec les fées des plaines
> Nous jetons des cailloux aux vers luisants
> Je suis le roi et vous êtes ma reine
> Et nous aurons un jour cent huit enfants.
> Jean répondit: "Je suis un homme arctique
> J'ai sept deux [sic] pieds et la queue d'un démon
> On a comblé la mer Adriatique
> Pour faire passer mon char et mes canons.
> ("Bourlinguer," DP, p. 14).

Here, fanciful mythology is put in the service of a whimsical anecdote combining fairy tale figures, antique armor, and imaginary numbers. The resultant anecdote constitutes fantasy rather than metaphor since the emphasis is on the anecdote. Metaphorical configurations such as those previously analysed, on the other hand, either attempt to make the unknown palpable, or to express a particular complex of emotions and meaning through a wholly self-contained image. Analysis can show how the image works but it cannot duplicate its effect, which is expressed only through the particular configuration of the image. The metaphor therefore constitutes an entirely new and unique semantic entity.

When metaphors succeed one another, a variety of relationships exist between the images which constitute the series. Each individual metaphor can be developed independently of the others in the series, and differently from it. The relationships among series of metaphors are analogous to those of other images analysed, in that each can modify the meaning of the preceding one, or the entire sequence can work as one unit.

When metaphors are enumerated, the series can juxtapose metaphors that illustrate the same theme:

> mes années sont des guerres de nations
> le bruit de mes années ce sont des bruits d'avion
> mes années de mémoire sont un bruit d'armes
> et chacune est le fils de la montagne
> mes années ont gardé l'empreinte de vos bottes
> noirs et noirs souvenirs qui parcourez mes grottes
> ("Poème," FddL, n. p.).

The unity of this passage derives from two factors. One is the repetition of "mes années." The other is that each of the metaphors is primarily affective, evoking the pain the speaker experiences when he remembers his past, whether through personification, choice of vacabulary ("noirs et noirs souvenirs"), or correspondences (the analogy between "années" and "guerres de nations," or "années" and "bruits d'avion," each suggesting a kind of discord or suffering). The metaphors do not modify each other explicitly; but each adds a new nuance, a somewhat different evocation of pain or discord, so that the total sequence expresses more than any of its individual components.

The metaphors in these enumerations can be less explicitly related. The opening sequence of the same poem is an example:

> Un cri perce une montagne de douleurs
> une sortie vers le Seigneur
> mes années sont des guerres de nations

As in the previous example, there is no punctuation. The first two lines must be read as one unit "une sortie" represents an extension and illustration of the first line, implying that the cry expresses not only despair, but through the realization of the despair, a reaching out towards the Deity. No transition exists between these two lines and the metaphor beginning with "mes années." The link must be supplied through the content of the image. The metaphor can be read as a causal one, giving the reasons for the despair of the lyrical "I" expressed in the first two lines. It can also be interpreted as an evocation of the same state of mind as is present in the first two lines. The juxtaposition of images whose relationship is not made explicit favors a multiplicity of interpretations.

In Jacob's poetry, there can also be a break in continuity between succeeding metaphors. The most violent contrasts are those between a humorous, nonsensical poem, and a final metaphor, which is lyrical, as in the poem entitled: "Ils ne reviendront plus," in CD, p. 167:

> Quand reviendront les fossoyeurs devant la tombe d'Ophélie? Ophélie n'est pas encore dans son immortelle tombe; ce sont les fossoyeurs qu'on y mettra si le cheval blanc le veut. Et le cheval blanc? il vient chaque jour brouter les cailloux. C'est le cheval blanc de l'auberge du Cheval-Blanc devant la tombe. Il a trente-six côtes. La tombe est une fenêtre ouverte sur le mystère.

Each sentence in this poem repeats a word from the previous sentence, but then goes off into a totally different direction, very much as in a *coq-à-l'âne*. The final metaphor, out of context, is both expressive and affective. But nothing in the poem prepares it. Similarly, in the following untitled poem from DP, p. 110, quoted in its entirety:

> Il y a des étoiles qui sont des abeilles, ambre foncé et onyx; d'autres sont des saphirs clairs.
>
> Dieu a les yeux clos.

the first metaphor initially suggests a visual analogy between bees, stars and precious stones, based on the color and texture of bee's bodies and the glow of precious stones and stars. The second image however, is totally unexpected, and totally obscure. Out of context, by itself, as a short poem, this image would not be hermetic. It might be taken as a symbol of the indifference of the Deity, or as a lyrical expression of despair, or as a pretty fantasy. The context, however, gives no clue as to whether any of these is appropriate. There is no transition between this image and the one preceding it, no relationship of any kind. Indeed, the break is so total, the second image so startling, that the initial interpretation of the first image retroactively is modified as the reader seeks to relate it to what follows. The linkage of two irreconcilable images within the same poem transforms the whole. The poem is not hermetic since each image is highly evocative. But the linear sequence of language, of syntax, is broken: the images must be read "backward and forward" so to speak, and the usual cognitive function of language is thereby totally altered. Words function at the level of the image, the suggestion, the sensation. The poem acts as a trigger upon the imagination as the reader focuses more and more intensely upon the images. The result is analogous, in a fundamental way, to the ambiguity of the poem analysed in the section on sound links: "L'enfant, l'éfant..." Again, interpretations may be invented which will justify the association between the two metaphors. Once more there is no justification for the poem other than itself and the feast it provides for the imagination.

CONCLUSION

I have based this study on a conception of poetry as a means of using language so that the communicative potential of words is renewed in some way: each device selected was analysed in this light. Throughout the book, I have repeatedly stressed two themes: that Jacob's poetry makes use of many devices or aspects of language which had been considered either apoetic or antipoetic because associated with "low" or "humorous" contexts; that it uses them to force a re-examination of the meaning of these words, to show them in a new light.

Throughout the book, I have stressed the differences between the various devices studied. Yet retrospectively, one notes many similarities as well. Chief among them is their creation of complexity of meaning. The difference between puns and metaphors lies not in the supposed frivolity of one as opposed to the power of revelation of the other; rather, each affects meaning in different ways. Puns focus on the multiple existing meaning of words. This device achieves great density by making it possible to compress within one utterance a number of seemingly unrelated meanings; or to contrast these meanings (in the case of paronomasia) in a particularly striking context. The result is an exploration of language in depth. Metaphors, on the other hand, create new meanings for words by encapsulating many meanings that cannot be expressed in other ways: it is impossible to paraphrase the full meaning of a metaphor. The result is an outward expansion of language. Midway between these two is the device I have called "substantives expressive in a number of ways at once." Characteristic of this device is the fact that the existing meanings of words, often drawn from the vernacular, are not altered. Commonplace objects are evoked concretely, yet they acquire additional overtones which may be affective, psychological, metaphysical, etc. Complexity of meaning can be signaled by rhetorical or syntactical devices; or, in the case of metaphors or puns, can result from the devices themselves. In Jacob's poetry, it also relates to a conception of the universe that is anachronistic to the twentieth century because it is based on occult beliefs that situate objects in the material world in a system of correspondences with a spiritual reality and attributing quasi-magical powers to them and perhaps to language as well. This conception of the universe becomes a source of imagery, as well as a means of transforming objects.

Complexity of meaning is also associated with ambiguity. Again, metaphor is the most complex example since it is impossible to paraphrase its full meaning, which is realized only in the particular image. Metaphor represents one pole where language is enriched. Yet here, the range is very broad. At another pole, with certain types of sound links, for example, words are seemingly emptied of cognitive meaning. The total structure of a poem can result in similar ambiguities. Some of the poems develop an internal logic based on the relationships of images or words to each other, often playful and fanciful, bearing little resemblance to the logic of the ordinary, rational, commonsense interpretation of reality or language. The result is analogous, at the level of the entire poem, to the re-examination of the meanings of individual words. In attempting to interpret poems that do not lend themselves to this type of logical, "commonsense" interpretation of language or reality, various types of reactions are experienced. At times causing simply frustration or disorientation, the poem leads to a number interpretations, none excluding the others, each, in pun fashion, relatively independent of the others. The text can also act as a trigger, forcing the invention of different solutions. At another extreme, the poem ceases to communicate any meaning that can be paraphrased in cognitive terms. A number of poetic structures have these various results; for example, a structural pattern seemingly at odds with the focus of the poem, or a profusion of details which do not seem to mesh or which seem to lead nowhere. Still another is the existence, in the poem, of irreconcilable manners, tones, or styles.

All of these can be associated equally with what I have called "creative paradies," sound links, or certain types of imagery. Ultimately, all these appeal to the imagination: such poems, like metaphors, are finally impervious to analysis.

All of these considerations bear witness to the artificiality of the distinctions between poetic and anti-poetic devices. Analysis of diction is particularly revealing: some of the examples cited in the chapter on sound and word play are based on rare vocabulary, or derive from traditional poetic diction, whereas some of the examples studied in the chapter on imagery use as their vehicle the most mundane, commonplace, or even repulsive aspects of reality. The reverse is also true. Jacob found his poetic material everywhere: whatever suits the logic of a poem is by definition poetic. Jacob, moreover, composed individual poems in the same way he composed his entire work: longer poems, are composites in which all or many of the devices studied are blended together.

This does not mean, however, that Jacob's poetry is indiscriminate, or that it lacks individuality and character. Jacob's imprint is unmistakable. His originality derives from the unique way in which the various devices are combined in his poetry to become one voice, one presence. At the level of language and structure, this voice is especially marked by the use of prosaic elements, nonsense, sound and word play, parodies; at the thematic level, by the extensive use of dream images, and the intrusion into the everyday of the supernatural. The exclusion from my anaysis of any biographical considerations does not mean that the world of Jacob is absent. On the contrary, Jacob's particular vision of reality must be referred to constantly: it is, however, contained in the poems themselves. It is, after all, his poetic universe which interests us. The world that emerges is one in which the familiar reveals itself as multi-layered, multi-dimensional; a world where there is no visible separation between myth, reality, and dream, where the commonplace is the supernatural, a little girl, the devil, and a cloud, an angel. The familiar, be it a familiar meaning, a familiar object, is transformed. Meaning, rationality, logic, nonsense are reinterpreted. Poetry dwells in the ordinary — and everywhere else.

Jacob's reputation as a poet, up to now, has primarily been that of an innovator, not a poet so much as, in the formula coined by Gabriel Bounoure, "un inventeur de poésie." Nevertheless, the variety of devices, as well as Jacob's mastery in utilising fully the resources of language, testify that his accomplishments are those of a poet of considerable stature. Jacob had considered calling the *Cornet à dès* "Poésies incomplètes," indicating that the texts need the active participation of the reader to become — fully — poems. He had also expressed the wish (in the Preface to that volume) that he be read not long, but often. It is hoped that this study will lead the reader back to the texts where he will ponder, and give life, through the imagination, to all of Jacob's "Poésies incomplètes."

BIBLIOGRAPHY: *LIST OF WORKS CONSULTED*

I have divided this bibliography into three sections. Section I, primary sources, consists of volumes or publications in periodicals written by Jacob. I have not attempted to compile an exhaustive bibliography, listing only those volumes or editions actually used in the preparation of this book.

Section II lists articles or volumes dealing specifically with Max Jacob's work. I have omitted articles or volumes which are of biographical interest only, as well as references to anthologies, general histories of literature, etc. that mention Jacob only in a passing way. For additional bibliographical data, see the general bibliographies of twentieth century French literature, such as *Talvart et Place, Thieme, French VII*. See also the bibliographies contained in vols. I, II, and V of the *Cahiers Max Jacob*, and in the special number of the periodical *Io*, entitled "Pour en revenir à Max Jacob," Paris, 1970; the bibliography contained pp. 192-205, of the *Serie Max Jacob* de la *Revue des Lettres Modernes, Cahier* No. 1, Aug. 1973; as well as the bio-bibliography in *Europe*, No. 348-49 (April-May 1958).

Section III lists articles or volumes relating to stylistics or to specific aspects of style considered in the book, as well as material containing general historical background.

I. PRIMARY SOURCES.

A Poèmes rompus. Paris: Louis Broder, 1960.
Art poétique. Paris: Emile Paul Frères, 1922.
Ballades. Paris: Nouvelles Editions Debresse, 1954.
———. Paris: Gallimard, 1970.
Billy, André. *Max Jacob, une étude, avec des lettres du poète à Guillaume Apollinaire et à Jean Cocteau, un choix de poèmes, des inédits, des manuscrits, des dessins, des portraits, une bibliographie*. Nouvelle édition refondue et augmentée. Paris: P. Seghers, 1945.
Bourgeois de France et d'ailleurs. Paris: Gallimard, 1932.
Le Cabinet noir. Lettres avec commentaires. Edition considérablement revue et augmentée. Paris: Gallimard, 1928.
———. Edition définitive, revue et augmentée de cinq lettres inédites. Gallimard, 1968.
Choix de lettres de Max Jacob à Jean Cocteau: 1919-1944. Paris: Editions Paul Morihien, 1949.

Chronique des temps héroïques. Illustrations by Picasso. Paris: Louis Broder, 1956.
Le Cinématoma. Fragments de mémoires des autres. Paris: Editions de la Sirène, 1920.
Conseils à un jeune poète, suivis de *Conseils à un étudiant.* Paris: Gallimard, 1945.
Le Cornet à dez. Poèmes en prose. Edition complète, revue et corrigée par l'auteur. Paris: Stock, 1923.
———. Paris: Editions Gallimard, Collection "Poésie," 1967.
———. Poèmes en prose. Paris: Gallimard, 1945.
Le Cornet à des, II. Poèmes en prose. Note liminaire d'André Salmon. Paris: Gallimard, 1955.
Correspondance. I. Quimper-Paris, 1900-21. François Garnier, ed. Paris: Editions de Paris, 1953.
———. II. St. Benoît-sur-Loire, 1921-24. François Garnier, ed. Paris: Editions de Paris, 1955.
La Côte. Recueil de chants celtiques inédits. Texte breton revue par M. J. Tanguy. Paris: Birault, 1911.
La Défense de Tartufe: extases, remords, visions, prières, poèmes et méditations d'un juif converti. Nouvelle édition. Introduction et notes par André Blanchet. Paris: Gallimard, 1964.
Derniers poèmes en vers et en prose. Paris: Gallimard, 1945.
Dos d'Arlequin. Théâtre. Paris: Kra, 1921.
Drawings and Poems. Translated and edited, with an introduction by S. J. Collier. New York: Lotus Press, 1951.
Esthétique de Max Jacob, par René Guy Cadou. Paris: P. Seghers, 1956.
Filibuth, ou la montre en or. Roman. Paris: Gallimard, 1923.
———. Paris: Gallimard, 1968.
Fond de l'eau. Poèmes. Paris: Editions les Cahiers Libres, 1927.
Histoire du Roi Kaboul Ier et du marmiton Gauwain. Conte. Préface d'André Salmon. Les Cahiers Max Jacob, I. Paris, March, 1951.
L'Homme de chair et l'homme reflet. Roman. Paris: Simon Kra, 1924.
L'Homme de cristal. Poèmes. Illustrations de l'auteur. Paris: Editions de la Table Ronde, 1946.
———. Edition revue et augmentée; note liminaire par Pierre Albert Birot. Paris: Gallimard, 1967.
Isabelle et Pantalon. Opéra-bouffe en deux actes de Max Jacob, musique de Roland Manuel. Paris: Au Ménestrel, 1922.
"J'en passe et des meilleures," [sketch signé "Morven le Gaelique,"] *NRF,* XXXVI (April 1, 1931), 593-7.
Kimball, Anne S. *Lettres de Max Jacob à Jouhandeau.* Unpublished dissertation, University of Wisconsin, 1969.
Le Laboratoire central. Poèmes. Paris: Au Sans Pareil, 1921.
———. Poèmes. Préface d'Yvon Belaval. Paris: Gallimard, 1960.
Lagarde, Pierre. *Max Jacob, mystique et martyr, avec trente deux méditations inédites, cinq poèmes, deux autographes, un dessin par Max Jacob.* Paris: Editions Baudinière, 1945.
Lettres, 1920-1941. A T. Briant et C. Valence. S. J. Collier, ed. Oxford, Blackwell, 1966.
Lettres à un ami [Jean Grenier]. Lausanne: Editions Vineta: 1951.

Lettres à Marcel Béalu, précédées de *Dernier visage de Max Jacob.* Lyon: Editions Emmanuel Vitte, 1959.
Lettres à Bernard Esdras-Gosse. Paris: Seghers, 1953.
Lettres aux Salacrou: août 1923-Janvier 1926. Paris: Gallimard, 1957.
Lettres imaginaires. Préface de Jean Cocteau. Les Cahiers Max Jacob, II. Paris, March 1952.
Max Jacob et la Bretagne, suivi de "La Couronne de Vulcain," conte breton, par Max Jacob. Les Cahiers Max Jacob, V. Paris, 1961.
Méditations religieuses. Préface et choix de l'Abbé Morel. Paris: Gallimard, 1947.
Méditations. Édition établie et présentée par René Plantier. Paris, 1972.
Miroir d'astrologie. En collaboration avec Claude Valence. Edition définitive contenant des extraits du Livre d'Arcandam, les analogies se rapportant à chaque contsellation, les correspondances astrologiques des lames du Tarot ainsi que des emblêmes proposés pour chaque signe et les Dames des Décans. Paris: Gallimard, 1949.
Morceaux choisis. Paris: Gallimard, 1936.
"Les Mots en liberté," *Nord-Sud,* No. 9 (Nov. 1917), 3-5.
Ne coupez pas, Mademoiselle ou les erreurs des P. T. T. Conte philosophique. Paris: Editions de la Galerie Simon, 1921.
"Le Nom," *Europe,* II, No. 7 (Aug. 1923), 385-96.
Le Nom. Nouvelles. Paris: Editions de la Sirène, 1926.
Les Œuvres burlesques et mystiques de Frère Matorel. Edition originale, illustrée de gravures sur bois par Derain. Paris: H. Kahnweiler, 1912.
Oxenhandler, Neil. "Max Jacob et les *Feux de Paris,*" *University of California Publications in Modern Philology.* XXXV, No. 4. Berkeley and Los Angeles: University of California Press, 1964, 221-308.
"Parmi vos lettres, Max [Lettres à Sylvette Fillacier]," *Europe,* 36ème année, No. 348-49 (April May 1958), 76-101.
Les Pénitents en maillots roses. Poèmes. Paris: Simon Kra, 1925.
Le Phanérogame. Paris: chez l'auteur, Imprimerie Levé, 1918.
Poèmes de Morven le Gaélique. Préface de Julien Lanoe. Paris: Gallimard, 1953.
Le Roi de Béotie. Nouvelles. Paris: Gallimard, 1921.
Le Roi de Béotie, suivie de La Couronne de Vulcain et de Hi toire du roi Kaboul 1er et du marmiton Gauwain. Edition définitive. Gallimard, 1971.
Romanesques. Nouvelles. Préface de François Mauraic. Les Cahiers Max Jacob, IV. Paris, 1954.
Saint Matorel. Edition originale illustrée d'eaux fortes par Picasso. Paris: H. Kahnweiler, 1911.
———. Roman, suivi des *Œuvres burlesques et mystiques de Frère Matorel, mort au couvent* et du *Siège de Jérusalem,* drame céleste. Paris: Gallimard, 1936.
Le Siège de Jérusalem. Grande Tentation céleste de St. Matorel. Edition originale illustrée d'eaux fortes par Pablo Picasso. Paris: H. Kahnweiler, 1914.
Tableau de la bourgeoisie. Portraits. Illustré de lithographies originales et de nombreux dessins par l'auteur. Paris: Gallimard, 1929.
Le Terrain Bouchaballe. Roman. Paris: Gallimard, 1964.

Théâtre, I. Un Amour du Titien, La Police Napolitaine. Préface de Henri Sauguet. Les Cahiers Max Jacob, III. Paris, March 1953.
Visions Infernales. Poèmes en prose. Paris: Gallimard, 1924.

II. BIBLIOGRAPHY CONCERNING MAX JACOB'S WORK.

Allard, Roger. "Le Laboratoire central, Dos d'Arlequin," *NRF*, XVII (Dec. 1, 1921), 743-746.
Andreu, Pierre. *Max Jacob.* Collection Conversions célèbres, dirigée par Gilbert Ganne. Paris: Wesmail Charlier, 1962.
Arland, Marcel. "L'Homme de chair et l'homme reflet," *NRF*, XXII (June 1, 1924), 747-48.
―――. "Le Terrain Bouchaballe," *NRF*, XXIII (Aug. 1, 1923), 228-30.
―――. "Visions infernales," *NRF*, XXIII (Sept. 1, 1924), 360.
Béalu, Marcel. *Dernier Visage de Max Jacob: 1937-1944.* Périgueux: P. Fanlac, 1946.
―――. "Max Jacob, poète," *Cahiers du Nord,* 22ème année, Nos. 3-4 (April 23, 1951), 196-204.
Belaval, Yvon. "Le Laboratoire central," *NRF*, 8ème année, No. 86 (Feb. 1960), 295-305.
―――. *La Rencontre avec Max Jacob.* Paris: Editions Charlot, 1946.
Billy, André. "Max Jacob," *Huysmans et Cie.* Paris: Nizet, 1962, 195-227.
Boschère, Jean de. "Une lettre de Jean de Boschère," *France-Asie,* III (April 1948), 520-9.
Bosquet, Alain. "Relire les poèmes de Max Jacob," *NRF*, No. 218 (Fev. 1971), 59-67.
Bounoure, Gabriel. "Les Pénitents en maillots roses, Visions infernales, Fond de l'eau, Rivages," *NRF*, XXXXIII (July 1, 1934), 109-19.
Bouret, Jean. "Deux Retrospectives: Max Jacob et Guillaumin," *Les Lettres Françaises,* No. 26 (Oct. 21, 1944).
Breunig, L. C. "Max Jacob et Picasso," *MF*, No. 1132 (Dec. 1957), 581-96.
Cadou, René Guy. "L'Œuvre de Max Jacob," *Cahiers du Nord,* 22ème année, Nos. 3-4 (April 21, 1951), 178-95.
Cassou, Jean, "Adieu à Max Jacob," *Cahiers du Sud,* No. 273 (2ème semestre 1945), 561-4.
―――. "Max Jacob et la liberté," *NRF*, XXX (April 1, 1928), 455-63.
Charensol, G. "Comment écrivez-vous? enquête," *Nouvelles Littéraires,* année 11 (Feb. 20, 1932), 5.
Collier, S. J. "The Correspondence of Max Jacob," *French Studies,* VII, No. 3 (July 1953), 235-56.
―――. "Max Jacob and the 'Poème en prose,'" *The Modern Language Review,* LI, No. 4 (Oct. 1956), 522-35.
―――. "Max Jocob's *Le Cornet à dés,*" *French Studies,* XI (April 1957), 149-67.
Duhamel, Georges. "Les Poèmes," *MF, CIII,* No. 384 (June 16, 1913), 800.
Emié, Louis. *Dialogues avec Max Jacob.* Paris: Corréa, 1954.
Fabureau, Hubert. *Max Jacob.* Paris: Editions de la Nouvelle Revue Critique, 1935.
Fontainas, André. "Le Laboratoire central," *MF*, CXLIX (Aux. 1, 1921), 739-40.

Fontainas, André. "Les Pénitents en maillots roses," MF, CLXXXVI (June 15, 1926), 671-2.

Fowlie, Wallace. "Hommage to Max Jacob," Poetry, LXXV, No. 6 (March 1950), 352-6.

Frick, Louis de Gonzague."M. Max Jacob et le 'Cornet à dés,'" SIC, No. 24 (Dec. 1917), n. p.

Gabory, Georges. "Le Roi de Béotie," NRF, XXXVIII (March 1, 1922), 347-8.

Ganzo, Robert. *Cinq Poètes assassinés: St. Pol Roux, Max Jacob, Robert Desnos, Benjamin Fondane et André Chennevières*. Paris: Editions de Minuit, 1948.

Garnier, François. "Max Jacob et le théâtre," Europe, No. 348-49 (April May 1958), 37-45.

Ghéon, Henri. "La Défense de Tartufe," NRF, 7ème année, No. 78 (March 1, 1920), 452-3.

Gourmont, Jean de. "Le Cinématoma," MF, CXLI, No. 529 (July 1, 1920), 182.

Grenier, Jean. "L'Art poétique de Max Jacob," Combat (Nov. 16, 1944), 6.

———. "Max Jacob," Aguedal, 4ème année, No. 2 (May 1939), 131-4.

Guégen, Pierre. "Rivage," Nouvelles Littéraires, année 11 (April 23, 1932), 5.

———. "Vie de Max Jacob," NRF, XLIII (July 1, 1934), 5-19 (August 1, 1934), 248-59.

Guillaume, Louis. "Max nous parle," France-Asie, III (March 15, 1948), 364-8.

Guilloux, Louis. "Max Jacob," France-Asie, III (March 15, 1948), 351-63.

Kamber, Gerald. "Max Jacob et Charles Baudelaire: une étude de sources," MLN, CLXXVIII (May 1963), 252-60.

———. *Max Jacob and the Poetics of Cubism* (Johns Hopkins Press: 1971).

Lannes, Roger. "Max Jacob," Poésie 44, No. 20 (July to Oct. 1944), 35-9.

———. "Max Jacob commenté par lui-même," Arts, No. 1 (Jan 31, 1945), 3.

Larnac, Jean. "Un Curieux Mystique," Le Divan, No. 252 (Oct. Dec. 1944), 392-4.

Lévy, Sydney. "Jeu et Poésie: Une Lecture du Cornet à dés de Max Jacob," Sub-Stance, No. 4 (Fall 1972), 27-44.

Magny, Olivier de. "Le Laboratoire central, par Max Jacob," Les Lettres Françaises, 8ème année, No. 7 (Oct. 1960), 179-80.

Malraux, André. "Art poétique, par Max Jacob," NRF, XIX (Aug. 1, 1922), 227-8.

Oberlé, Jean. "Max Jacob, poète et martyr," La France Libre, No. 44 (June 15, 1944), 102-4.

Olivier, Fernande. *Picasso et ses amis*. Paris: Stock, 1933.

Otten, Arthur. *Max Jacob: La Formation et la nature de son art*. Unpublished dissertation, Université de Laval, 1970.

Palacio, Jean de. "Max Jacob et Apollinaire: documents inédits," Studi Francesi, No. 42 (1970), 467-74.

———. "Un Précurseur inattendu de Max Jacob: Lord Byron," Revue de Littérature comparée (1970), 187-207.

Parrot, Louis. "Pour comme un Enfant, le souvenir de Max Jacob," Les Lettres Françaises, No. 45 (March 3, 1945).

Parturier, Maurice. "Max Jacob," Le Divan, No. 252 (Oct. Dec. 1944), 395-404.

Pia, Pascal. "Etudes jacobiennes," *Carrefour*, No. 1018 (March 18, 1964), 20.
———. "Filibuth, *NRF*, XXII (May 1, 1923), 833-5.
Plantier, René. *Max Jacob*. Desclée de Brouwer, 1972.
Rousselot, Jean. "Contribution à une esthétique de Max Jacob," *Revue d'esthétique*, tome X, fasc. 3 (July-Sept. 1957), 296-318.
———. "Max Jacob," *Cahiers du Nord*, 22ème année, Nos. 3-4 (April 23, 1951), 205-10.
———. *Max Jacob, l'homme qui faisait penser à Dieu: essai*. Paris: Robert Laffont, 1946.
———. "Max Jacob ou le sel dans la plaie," *Présences contemporaines: Rencontres sur le chemin de la poésie*. Paris: Nouvelles Editions Debresse, 1958, 127-140.
———. *Max Jacob au sérieux*. Rodez: Editions Subervie, 1958.
———. "Poète et martyr," *Les Nouvelles Littéraires*, 42ème année, No. 1906 March 12, 1964), 2.
Salmon, André, "Cinq-Mars," *France-Asie*, III (March 15, 1948), 353-6.
———. *Max Jacob, poète, peintre, mystique et homme de qualité*. Paris: René Girard, 1927.
———. *La Negresse du Sacré Cœur*. Roman. Paris: Gallimard, 1920. (Jacob is pictured under the name Septime Fébur).
Sauguet, Henri. "Max Jacob et la musique," *Revue Musicale*, No. 210 (Jan, 1952), 151-4.
Schneider, Judith M., "Max Jacob on Poetry," *The Modern Language Review*, Vol. 69, No. 2 (April 1974), 291-296.
Simon, Pierre Henri. "Max Jacob: La Défense de Tartufe, Le Terrain Bouchaballe," *Le Monde*, No. 807 (April 2-8, 1964), 11.
Szigeti, Robert. "Amitié de Max Jacob," *Europe*, No. 348-49 (April May 1958), 32-7.
Thau, Annette. "The Esthetic Reflections of Max Jacob," *The French Review*, Vol. 45, No. 4, March 1972.
———. Poetry and Anti Poetry: A Study of Selected Aspects of Max Jacob's Poetic Style, with an introduction to his esthetics. Unpublished dissertation. Columbia University, 1967.

The following periodicals published special numbers about Max Jacob:
Le Disque Vert, No. 2 (Nov. 1923).
Le Mail, No. 5 (April 1928).
L'Année Poétique, No. 2 (Jan. 1934).
Aguedal, 4ème année, No. 2 (May 1939).
Le Val D'Or, "Max Jacob, le poète pénitent de St. Benoit," (Feb. 1945).
La Boite à Clous, "Hommage à Max Jacob," (Bordeaux, Feb. 1951).
Simoun, "Tombeau de Max Jacob," Nos. 17-18 (Oran, 1955).
Europe, No. 348-49 (April-May 1958).
Iô, "Pour en revenir à Max Jacob," (Paris, 1970).
La Revue des Lettres Modernes, Nos. 336-339 (Paris, 1973). *Max Jacob*, I.

III. GENERAL REFERENCES.

Adank, Hans. *Essai sur les Fondements psychologiques et linguistiques de la métaphore affective*. Genève: Imprimerie et Editions Union, S. A., 1939.

Aegerter Emmanuel et Pierre Labracherie. *Au Temps de Guillaume Apollinaire*. Paris: René Julliard, 1945.
Aish, Deborah Amelia Kirk. *La Métaphore dans l'œuvre de Stéphane Mallarmé*. Paris: Droz, 1938.
Amour, L. M. "Le Pastiche et la parodie chez Jules Lemaître," *CAIEF*, No. 12 (June 1960), 15-29.
Antoine, Gérald. *Les Cinq Grandes Odes de Claudel; ou la poésie de la répétition*. Paris: M. J. Minard, Lettres Modernes, 1959.
———. "Pour une Méthode d'analyse stylistique des images," *Actes de VIIIème Congrès de la Fédération Internationale des Langues et Littératures modernes*. Paris: Société d'Edition "Les Belles Lettres," 1961, 151-164.
Auerbach, Erich. "The Esthethic Dignity of the *Fleurs du mal*," in Henri Peyre, ed., *Baudelaire, a Collection of Critical Essays*. Englewood Cliffs: Prentice Hall, 1962, 150-160.
———. *Mimesis: The Representation of Reality in Western Literature*. New York: Doubleday Anchor Books, 1953.
Bachelard, Gaston. *L'Eau et les rêves: Essai sur l'imagination de la matière*. Paris: J. Corti, 1941.
———. *La Psychanalyse du feu*. Paris: Gallimard, 1965.
Balakian, Anna. "André Breton et l'hermétisme: des *Champs magnétiques* à la *Clé des champs*," *CAIEF*, No. 15 (March 1963), 221-237.
———. "La Langue surréaliste," *Actes du VIIIème Congrès de la Fédération Internationale des Langues et Littératures modernes*. Paris: Société d'Edition "Les Belles Lettres," 1961, 238-9.
———. *Literary Origins or Sureralism: a New Mysticism in French Poetry*. New York: King's Crown Press, 1947.
———. *Surrealism: the Road to the Absolute*. New York: Noonday Press, 1959.
———. "The Surrealist Image," *Romanic Review*, XLIV (Dec. 1953), 273-280.
Bousquet, Jacques. *Les Thèmes du rêve dans la littérature romantique: essai sur la naissance et l'évolution des images*. Paris: Didier, 1964.
Buchole, Rosa. *L'Evolution poétique de Robert Desnos*. Bruxelles: publ. of the Académie Royale de Langues et Littératures françaiess de Belgique, 1956.
Burke, Kenneth. "Four Master Tropes (metaphor, metonymy, synecdoche, and irony)," *A Grammar of Motives*. New York: Peter Smith, 1946, 503-17.
Butor, Michel. "Esquisse d'un seuil pour Finnegan," *NRF*, Année 5, Tome X (Dec. 1, 1957), 1033-53.
Carco, Francis. *Les Humoristes*. Paris: Librairie Paul Ollendorf, 1921.
———. *De Montmartre au Quartier Latin*. Paris: Editions Albin Michel, 1927.
Carmody, F. T. *Cubist Poetry of the School of Apollinaire, 1912-1919*. Mimeographed pamphlet, 1952.
Chapelan, Maurice. *Anthologie du poème en prose; introduciton, choix et notes de Maurice Chapelan*. Paris: R. Julliard, 1946.
Chérel, A. *La Prose poétique française*. Paris, 1940.
Chevalier, J. C. "Apollinaire et le calembour," *Europe*, Année 44, 551-2 (Nov. Dec. 1966), 56-76.

Cocteau, Jean. *Poésie critique*. 2 vols. Paris: Gallimard, 1960.
——. *Le Rappel à l'ordre*. Paris: Stock, 1926.
Cohen, Jean. *Structure du langage poétique*. Paris: Flammarion, 1966.
Coomaraswamy, Amanda K. "Intention," *American Bookman*, I (1944), 41-48.
Corbière, Tristan. *Œuvres choisies*. Paris: Seghers, 1951.
Courville, M. Xavier de. "Pastiche et parodie chez Jules Lemaître," *CAIEF*, No. 12 (June 1960), 31-41.
Bally, Charles. *Traité de stylistique françai e*. Genève: George et Cie., 1951.
Bar, Francis. "Style burlesque et genre populaire," *CAIEF*, I, No. 9 (June 1957), 221-237.
Barfield, Owen. *Poetic Diction: a Study in Meaning*. London: Faber and Faber, 1928.
Baudelaire, Charles. *Œuvres Complètes*. Bibliothèque de la "Pléiade." Paris: Gallimard, 1954.
Baum, Paul F. "Chaucer's Puns," *PMLA*, LXXI (1956), 225-246.
Belaval, Yvon. *La Recherche de la poésie*. Paris: Gallimard, 1947.
Berge, André. *L'Esprit de la littérature moderne*. Paris: Perrin et Cie., 1939.
Bergson, Henri. *Le Rire. Essai sur la signification du comique*. Paris: Félix Alcan, 1900.
Bernard, Suzanne. *Le Poème en prose de Baudelaire jusqu'à nos jours*. Paris: Librairie Nizet, 1959.
Billy, André. *L'Epoque contemporaine, 1905-1950*. Paris: Editions Jules Tallandier, 1956.
Blanchot, Maurice. *L'Espace littéraire*. Paris: Gallimard, 1955.
Black, Max. *Models and Metaphors*. Ithaca: Cornell University Press, 1962.
Breton, André. *Anthologie de l'humour noir*. Paris: Editions du Sagittaire, 1940.
——. *Les Manifestes du surréalisme, suivis de Prolégomènes à un troisième manifeste du surréalisme ou non du surréalismo en ses œuvres vives et d'éphémères surréalistes*. Paris: Le Sagittaire, 1955.
Breunig, L. C. "Apollinaire et le monostique, communication aux Journées Apollinaire de Stavelot," *Académie Royale de Langue et Littérature françaises* (August 31, 1963), 1-13.
Brown, James. "Eight Types of Puns," *PMLA*, LXXI (1956), 14-26.
Bruneau, Charles. "Langue populaire," *CAIEF*, I, No. 9 (June 1957), 238-249.
Bounoure, Gabriel. *Marelles sur le parvis; essais de critique poétique*. Paris: Plon, 1958.
Cressot, Marcel. *Le Style et ses techniques*. Paris: Presses Universitaires de France, 1959.
Décaudin, M. *La Crise des valeurs symbolistes: 20 ans de poésie française, 1895-1914*. Toulouse: Editions Privat, 1960.
——. "Obscurité et composition chez Apollinaire," *CAIEF*, No. 15 (March 1963), 119-125.
Deffoux, León. *Le Pastiche littéraire*. Paris: Dumoulin, 1926.
——. *Le Pastiche littéraire des origines à nos jours*. Paris: Delagrave, 1932.
Delbouille, Paul. *Poésie et sonorités; la critique contemporaine devant le pouvoir suggestif des sons*. Paris: Les Belles Lettres, 1961.

Dermée, Paul. "Quand le symbolisme fut mort," *Nord-Sud*, No. 1 (March 15, 1917), 5-7.
"Dialogue nunique: A et B devant la painture moderne," Anon. series of articles, *SIC*, Nos. 5 (May 1916), n. p. through No. 18 (June 1917), n. p.
Durand, Gilbert. *Les Structures anthropologiques de l'imaginaire; introduction à l'archétypologie générale*. Grenoble: Imprimerie Allier, 1960.
Durry, Marie-Jeanne. *Jules Laforgue; avec choix de poèmes, bibliographie, desseins, portraits, fac-similés, textes inédits*. Paris: Seghers, 1952.
———. "Ombre-lumière dans la poésie de Guillaume Apollinaire," *MF*, CCCXXXVI (1959), 252-71.
Empson, William. *Seven Types of Ambiguity*. 2nd. edition. London: Chatto and Windus, 1947.
Fongaro, Antoine. "La Poétique de Pierre Reverdy," *Cahiers du Sud*, Année 41, No. 327 (Feb. 1955), 266-286.
Foster, Genevieve W. "The Archetypal Imagery of T. S. Elliot," *PMLA*, LX (1945), 567-85.
Frappier, Jean. "Aspects de l'hermétisme dans la poésie médiévale," *CAIEF*, No. 15 (March 1963), 9-24.
Frye, Northrop. *Anatomy of Criticism: Four Essays*. New York: Atheneum, 1966.
———. *Fearful Symmetry: A Study of William Blake*. Princeton: Princeton University Press, 1947.
———. "Three Meanings of Symbolism," *Yale French Studies*, No. 9 (1952), 11-19.
Garapon, Robert. *La Fantaisie verbale et le comique dans le théâtre français du Moyen Age à la fin du XVIIIème siècle*. Paris: Armand Colin, 1957.
Gill, André. "Les Vrais Bosquets de la Prose pour Des Esseintes," *CAIEF*, No. 15 (March 1963), 86-102.
Graves, Robert. *The Greek Myths*. 2 vols. Baltimore: Penguin Books, 1959.
Greet, Ann Hyde. *Humor as a Poetic Technique from Musset to Prévert*. Unpublished Dissertation. University of Colorado, 1961. Ann Arbor, Michigan: University Microfilms, 1961.
Grubbs, Henry A. "Nonsense in France and in French Literature," *Modern Language Quarterly*, VIII (1947), 21-9.
Gershman, Herbert. "Valéry, Breton and Eluard on Poetry," *French Review*, XXXVIII, No. 1 (Oct. 1964), 331-6.
Guiette, Robert. "L'Invention étymologique dans les lettres françaises au Moyen Age," *CAIEF*, No. 20 (June 1960), 43-52.
Guyard, Marie-François. "Claudel et l'étymologie," *CAIEF*, No. 11 (May 1959), 286-300.
Guyot, M. Charly. "Du Pastiche au faux: un pasticheur suisse français du XVIIIème siècle: Abram Pury," *CAIEF*, No. 20 (June 1960), 43-52.
Hubert, Renée Riese. "L'Evolution du poème en prose dans l'œuvre de Pierre Reverdy," *MLN*, LXXV, No. 3 (March 1960), 233-239.
———. "Le Langage de la peinture dans le poème en prose contemporain," *Revue des Sciences Humaines*, Fasc. 105 (Jan. March 1962), 109-116.
Huguet, Edmond. *Les Métaphores et les comparaisons dans l'œuvre de Victor Hugo*. 2 vols. Paris: Hachette, 1904-05.
Hrushowski, Benjamin. "On Free Rhythms in Modern Poetry," in Sebeok, Thomas A., ed., *Style in Language*. Published jointly by the Technology Press of M. I. T. and John Wiley and Sons, Inc., New York, London, 1960, 172-190. (Includes a brief bibliography on the subject, pp. 176-7.)

Jakobson, Roman. "Les Chats de Charles Baudelaire," *L'Homme: Revue Française d'Anthropologie*, II (1962), 5-21.
———. "Linguistics and Poetics," in Sebeok, Thomas A., ed., *Style in Language*. Published jointly by the Technology Press of M. I. T. and John Wiley and Sons, Inc., New York, London, 1960, 350-377.
Jakobson, Roman and Morris Halle. *Fundamentals of Language*. 's — Gravenhage: Mouton, 1956.
Jodogne, Omer. "La Parodie et le pastiche dans Aucassin et Nicolette," *CAIEF*, No. 12 (June 1960), 53-65.
Jones, Percy Mansell. *The Background of Modern French Poetry: Essays and Interviews*. Cambridge, Eng.: University Press, 1951.
Joyce, James. *The Dubliners*. New York: Modern Library, 1954.
Kies, Albert. "Imitation et pastiche dans l'œuvre de Charles Nodier," *CAIEF*, No. 12 (June 1960), 67-77.
Knights, L. C. and Basil Cottle, eds. *Metaphor and Symbol*. Proceedings of the Twelfth Symposium of the Colston Research Society held in the University of Bristol. London, 1960.
Kokeritz, Helge. "Rhetorical Word Play in Chaucer," *PMLA*, LXIX (1954), 937-52.
Konrad, Edwig. *Etude sur la métaphore*. Paris, 1958.
Langer, Susanne K. *Philosophy in a New Key: A Study in the Symbolism of Reason, Rite, and Art*. New York: Mentor Books, 1958.
Lawler, James R. "Music and Poetry in Apollinaire," *French Studies*, X, No. 4 (Oct. 1956), 339-46.
Le Dantec, Yves. "Sur le Poème en prose," *La Revue des Deux Mondes* (Oct. 15, 1948), 760-766.
Lefèvre, Frédéric. *La Jeune Poésie française, hommes et tendances*. Paris: Editions G. Crès et Cie., 1918.
———. *Une Heure avec....* Paris: Gallimard, 1924.
Le Hir, Yves. *Esthétique et structure du vers français d'après les théoriciens du XVIème siècle à nos jours*. Paris: Presses Universitaires de France, 1956.
Lemaître, G. *From Cubism to Surrealism in French Literature*. Cambridge, Mass.: Howard University Press, 1941.
Le Sage, Laurence. "Metaphor in the Non Dramatic Works of Jean Giraudoux," *University of Oregon Monographs: Studies in Literature and Philosophy*. Eugene, Oregon, Jan. 1952.
Levin, Samuel R. *Linguistic Structures in Poetry*. The Hague, Netherlands: Mouton and Co., 1962.
Mallarmé, Stéphane. *Poésies*. Paris: Gallimard, 1945.
Malraux, André. "Des Origines de la poésie cubiste," *Connaissance*, Année 1 (Jan. 1920), 38-43.
Marouzeau, Jules. *Précis de stylistique française*. Paris: Masson et Cie., 1950.
Mauron, Charles. *Des Métaphores obsédantes au mythe personnel: introduction à la psychocritique*. Paris: J. Corti, 1963.
Menemencioglu, Melâhat. "L'Automatisme psychique dans le poème hermétique," *CAIEF*, No. 15 (March 1963), 141-50.
Michaud, Guy. *Le Message poétique du symbolisme*. Paris: Nizet, 1961.
Monnerot, Jules. *La Poésie moderne et le sacré*. Paris: Gallimard, 1945.
Moré, Marcel. "Les Jeux de mots dans l'œuvre de Jules Verne," *Lettres Nouvelles*, CLI-CLV (1957), 711-30.
Murry, John Middleton. "Metaphor," *Countries of the Mind: Essays in Literary Criticism*. Second Series. London: Oxford University Press, 1931.

Nadeau, Maurice. *Histoire du surréalisme.* Paris: Editions du Seuil, 1945.
Parent, Monique. "La Langue du poème en prose," *Programme du Centre de Philologie Romane et de langue et littérature françaises contemporaines de Strasbourg* (1957), 45-50.
―――. *Rythme et versification dans la poésie de Francis Jammes.* Paris: Les Belles Lettres, 1957.
―――. *St. John Perse et quelques devanciers: études sur le poème en prose.* Paris: C. Klincksiek, 1960.
Paulhan, Jean. *Clef de la poésie qui permet de distinguer le vrai du faux en toute observation ou doctrine touchant la rime, le rythme, le vers et la poésie.* Nouvelle édition. Paris: Gallimard, 1962.
―――. *Les Fleurs de Tarbes ou la terreur dans les lettres.* Paris: Gallimard, 1941.
―――. *Jacob Cow le Pirate ou si les mots sont des signes.* Paris: Au Sans Pareil, 1921.
―――. *Petite préface à toute critique.* Paris: Editions de Minuit, 1951.
Peyre, Henri, ed. *Baudelaire, A Collection of Critical Essays.* Englewood Cliffs: Prentice Hall, 1962.
Picon, Gaetan. *Panorama des idées contemporaines.* Paris: Gallimard, 1957.
Piron, Maurice. "Lecture de Verlaine: 'Le Ciel est par-dessus le toit...,'" *French Studies,* X (1956), 32-9.
Raymond, Marcel. *De Baudelaire au surréalisme.* Nouvelle édition revue et remaniée. Paris: J. Corti, 1952.
Read, Herbert. "Obscurity in Poetry," *Collected Essays in Literary Criticism.* 2nd. edition. London: Faber and Faber, 1950, 89-100.
Renou, Louis. "Art et religion dans la poétique sanskrite: le jeu de mots et ses implications," *Journal de Psychologie Normale et Pathologique,* Nos. 1-2 (Jan. June 1951), 280-5.
Riffaterre, Michael. "Criteria for Style Analysis," *Word,* XV (1959), 154-74.
―――. "Describing poetic structures: Two approaches to Baudelaire's *les Chats,*" *Yale French Studies,* No. 36-37 (*Structuralism,* 1966), 200-242.
―――. *Essais de stylistique structurale.* Présentation et traductions par Daniel Delas. Paris: Flammarion, 1971.
―――. "L'Etude stylistique des formes conventionnelles," *The French Review,* XXXVIII, No. 1 (Oct. 1964), 3-14.
―――. "Fonctions du cliché dans la prose littéraire," *CAIEF,* No. 16 March 1964), 81-95.
―――. "Giraudoux: Irony and Poetry," *The American Society Legion of Honor Magazine,* XXIX, No. 1 (1958), 9-20.
―――. "Problèmes d'analyse du style littéraire," *Romance Philology,* XIV (1961), 216-27.
―――. *Le Style des Pléiades de Gobineau: essai d'application d'une méthode stylistique.* New York: Columbia University Press, 1957.
―――. "Stylistic Context," *Word,* XVI (1960), 207-18.
Rimbaud, Arthur. *Œuvres complètes.* Bibliothèque de la "Pléiade." Paris: Gallimard, 1954.
Rousselot, Jean. *Les Nouveaux Poètes français; panorama critique.* Paris: Seghers, 1959.
Salmon, André. *Souvenirs sans fin.* 3 vols. Paris: Gallimard, 1955-61.
Saporta, S. "The Application of Linguistics to the Study of Poetic Language," in Sebeok, Thomas A., ed. *Style in Language.* Published jointly by the Technology Press of M. I. T. and John Wiley and Sons, New York, London, 82-93.

Sayce, R. A. *Style in French Prose*. Oxford: Clarendon Press, 1953.
Sebeok, Thomas A., ed. *Style in Language*. Published jointly by the Technology Press of M. I. T. and John Wiley and Sons, Inc., New York, London, 1960.
Shattuck, Roger. *The Banquet Years: The Arts in France, 1885-1918; Alfred Jarry, Henry Rousseau, Erik Satie, Guillaume Apollinaire*. Garden City: Doubleday Anchor Books, 1961.
Siohan, Robert. "Les Formes musicales de la parodie et du pastiche," *CAIEF*, No. 12 (June 1960), 79-90.
Slote, Bernice, ed. *Myth and Symbol: Critical Approaches and Applications*. A Selection of papers delivered at the joint meeting of the Midwest Modern Language Association and the Central Renaissance Conference, 1962. Lincoln: University of Nebraska Press, 1963.
Sonnenfeld, Albert. "Calembour et création poétique chez Tristan Corbière," *Actes du VIIIème Congrès de la Fédération Internationale des langues et littératures modernes*. Paris: Société d'Edition "Les Belles Lettres," 1961, 392-3.
———. "Corbière: l'innovateur poétique," *L'Œuvre Poétique de Tristan Corbière*. Princeton: Princeton University Press, 1960.
Spitzer, Leo. *Linguistics and Literary History: Essays in Stylistics*. New York: Russell & Russell, Inc, 1962.
Spurgeon, Caroline F. E. *Shakespeare's Imagery and What it Tells Us*. Cambridge, Eng.: The University Press, 1961.
Staub, Hans. "Scève, poète hermétique," No. 15 (March 1963), 24-40.
Ullmann, Stephen. "L'Image littéraire: quelques questions de méthode," *Actes du VIIIème Congrès de la Fédération Internationale des langues et littératures modernes*. Paris: Société d'Edition "Les Belles Lettres," 1961, 41-60.
———. *The Image in the Modern French Novel: Gide, Alain-Fournier, Proust, Camus*. New York: Barnes and Noble, 1963.
———. *Language and Style, Collected Papers*. New York: Barnes and Noble, 1963.
———. *The Principles of Semantics*. 2nd. ed. New York: Barnes and Noble, 1957.
———. *Style in the French Novel*. New York: Barnes and Noble, 1964.
Valéry, Paul. "Au Sujet du Cimetière marin," and "Questions de poésie," *Variété III*. Paris: Gallimard, 1936.
Vigée, Claude. "L'Invention poétique et l'automatisme mental," *MLN*, LXXV, No. 2 (Feb. 1960), 143-54.
Voisine, Jacques. "Amphitryon, sujet de parodie," *CAIEF*, No. 12 (June 1960), 91-101.
Walcutt, Charles Child. "Critic's Taste and Artist's Intention," *The University of Kansas City Review*, XII (1946), 278-83.
Weber, Henri. "Y-a-t'il une poésie hermétique en France au XVIème siècle?" *CAIEF*, No. 15 (March 1963), 41-58.
Weber, Jean Paul. *Genèse de l'œuvre poétique*. Paris: Gallimard, 1960.
Wellek, René and Austin Warren. *Theory of Literature*. New York: Harcourt Brace and Company, 1956.
Wimsatt, William Kurtz, Jr. and Monroe C. Beardsley. *The Verbal Icon*. Lexington: The University of Kentucky Press, 1954.

LIST OF POEMS ANALYSED

The following is a complete list of poems analysed wholly or in part in this study. Untitled poems are identified by the opening words of the poem (in the case of brief one or two sentence poems), or of the passage analysed, and alphabetised accordingly.

(Untitled) "A ceci vous reconnaîtrez...," DP, 121	81
Acte de reconnaissance, HdC, 152	97
(Untitled) "Adam et Eve...," CD, 240	65
A Monsieur Modigliani pour lui prouver que je suis un poète, LC, 70.	60
Angoisses et autres, FddL, n. p., ...	31; 103
(Untitled) "L'Archange foudroyé...," CD, 57	84
Arrivée du démon, CD, II, 164	80
L'Art ariste, CD, I, 118	33
(Untitled) "L'Artillerie du Sacré Cœur...," CD, 59	27
Avenue du Maine, SM, 229	40
Avril infernal, DP, 27	74
Bourlinguer, DP, 14	107
(Untitled) "Brazéro, zéro... (Le)," CD, 64	39; 42
(Untitled) "Brouillard, étoile...," CD, 51	27
(Untitled) "Buisson d'épines... (Un)," CD, 54	95
Cancale, le crépuscule, LC, 85	101
Capitale: tapis de table, CD, 44	40
(Untitled) "Cet Allemand était fou d'art...," CD, 69	41; 44
Le Citadin mort à l'amour de la nature lui adresse ses adieux, LC, 74.	55
(Untitled) "Comme un bateau...," LC, 101	36
Conscience, CD, II, 174	95
Conte de Noël, CD, 76	62
(Untitled) "Ici la neige...," HdC, 138	29
(Untitled) "Il admirait...," LC, 183	101
(Untitled) "Il arrive quand tu ronfles," CD, 53	79
Ils ne reviendront plus, CD, 167	108
(Untitled) "Il y a des étoiles...," DP, 110	109
Incendie, CD, II, 102	86
(Untitled) "J'ai un mari...," CD, I, 238	34
(Untitled) "J'ai revu...," CD, 61	38

LIST OF POEMS ANALYSED

Marcel Proust, CD, II, 18	63
(Untitled) "Ma Séléné à moi...," CD, 65	43
Méli-mélo, CD, 190	92
(Untitled) "Mes grelots, maigre lot...," VI, 27	34
Métaphysique, 6, SI, MC, 98	34
Misère, CD, II, 173	83
Monde est au diable (Le), VI, 79	84
Mort (La), HdC, 159, 161, 164	39; 75; 104
Musique acidulée, LC, 169	48
Mystique noire, CD, II, 47	84
Nocturne, CD, II, 49	85
Nom (Le), CD, 128	62
Nouveau Baptême, HdC, 45	32
Nuit, FddL, n. p.	83; 102
Nuit Infernale, CD, 73	85
(Untitled) "On vient nous arrêter...," SM, 273	88
(Untitled) "Pan de ciel bleu... (Un)," CD, 66	94
Paradis et enfer, SI, MC, 99	29
Paralysie — parasitisme, CD, 81	40
Pardon la nuit en Bretagne, HdC, 41	32
Péché dans la recherche de la vertu, DT, 116	81
Peinture, CD, II, 187	77
Petit Essai sur le diable, CD, II, 52	24
Plainte du mauvais garçon, LC, 62	75
Plus d'Astrologie, LC, 115	100
Poème, CD, 38	25
Poème, CD, 44	90
Poème, FddL, n. p.	107
Corpus Christi, FddL, n. p.	96
Cygne (Le) [Genre essai plein d'esprit], CD, 91	40
Déménagement de la sacristie, DP, 139	34
Départ (Le), LC, 56	75
Dernier Calembour (Le), HdC, 97-98	26
Désigné, VI, 77	83
De Terre en ciel, HdC, 20	25
Deux Exercices d'exotisme, SM, 233	54
Ecrit pour la S. A. F., DT, 89	33
Effet de lune, LC, 98	28
Encore le roman feuilleton, CD, 124	66
(Untitled) "L'Enfant, l'éfant, l'éléphant...," CD, 55	45
L'Enfer est gradué, VI, 32	85
Enterrement à Quimper, DP, 53, 55	100
Equatoriales solitaires, CD, 152	40
Esprit de Raymond Radiguet, FddL, n. p.	96
Fausses Nouvelles! Fosses Nouvelles!, CD, 25	67
France (La), CD, II, 169	98

Guerre (La), CD, 24 ... ...   85; 87
Guerres et Amériques, DP, 196   79

Honneur de la Sardane et de la ténora, LC, 52, 54   92
Poème déclamatoire, CD, 36   54
Poème dans un goût qui n'est pas le mien, CD, 29, 30   53
Poème du Java de M. René Ghil et s'appelant less Ksours, CD, 72 ...   54
Poème de la lune, CD, 71   95
Présence de Dieu, DP, 93   93
(Untitled) "Princesse habitait (Une)...," CD, 241   65
Purgatoire, HdC, 70   76

Rebâtissons, DP, 118   29
Roman d'aventures, CD, 128   62
Roman feuilleton, CD, 89   62
Roman policier (Poème mystique), CD, II, 155   90
(Untitled) "Rue Ordener...," SM, 276   85

(Untitled) "Sabots pour dames (Des)...," DP, 194   86
Sacrifice d'Abraham (Le), CD, 141   37
Science lunarienne, CD, II, 15   79
Séjour, VI, 53   87
Sir Élizabeth (Prononcez sœur), CD, 120   64
Symbole artistique, CD, II, 39   78

Taie divine, DP, 74   103
Temps de révolution, CD, II, 133   89
Terre (La), SI, MC, 101   102
Terre arrosée, LC, 88   23
Thème de l'illusion et de l'amour, LC, 135   94
(Untitled) "Toit, c'est quatre... (Le)," CD, 63 ... ...   41; 44
Traduit de l'Allemand ou du Bosniaque, CD, 77   53

Une de mes Journées, CD, 176   57

Variation d'une formule, SM, 229   34
Ver ou serpent, CD, II, 34   32
Vers sans art, DP, 72 ... ...   91; 98
Vie et marée, CD, 183   53
Vie d'étudiant (La), CD, 154   63
Voisinage, VI, 55   85
Voyages, CD, 121   89
Vraie Jeunesse (La), DP, 38 ... ...   33; 92; 96

Yeux au ventre (Les), FddL, n. p.   95

The Department of Romance Studies Digital Arts and Collaboration Lab at the University of North Carolina at Chapel Hill is proud to support the digitization of the North Carolina Studies in the Romance Languages and Literatures series.

www.ingramcontent.com/pod-product-compliance
Lightning Source LLC
Chambersburg PA
CBHW030237240426
43663CB00037B/1245